A CONCISE DICTIONARY OF ARCHITECTURE

Frederic H. Jones, Ph.D

CRISP PUBLICATIONS, INC.
Los Altos, California

A CONCISE DICTIONARY OF ARCHITECTURE

Frederic H. Jones, Ph.D

CREDITS
Editor in Chief: **Frederic H. Jones, Ph.D**
Associate Editor: **Regina Sandoval**
Contributing Editors: **Linda Sandoval**
Judith Jones
William J. Fielder

Copyright © 1990 by Frederic H. Jones, Ph.D
Printed in the United States of America

Library of Congress Catalog Card Number 91-70351
Jones, Frederic H., Ph.D.
A Concise Dictionary of Interior Design
ISBN 1-56052-067-1

INTRODUCTION

Concise Dictionary of Architecture

This project has truly been a labor of love. Words have been a fascination for me all my life. I have collections of dictionaries, glossaries, word lists, etc. in many languages and on many subjects. I suppose it was just a matter of time before I was compelled to undertake a word list project of my own. I hope you find it both interesting and useful.

Many of the words and definitions included here were provided by historic dictionaries of architecture and design including the late 19th century edition by Russell Sturgis. Many of the illustrations have also been derived from these sources. In all cases the language and definitions were updated when necessary. Another primary source of words and their definitions were various associations and trade organizations. They include: The Illumination Engineering Society, Carpet and Rug Institute, Western Institute of Cabinetmakers, and many others. I wish to acknowledge their invaluable assistance and hasten to add that errors, no doubt, derive from my translation rather than from their creation.

My hope is that this and the other dictionaries in the series serve as introductory aids to students of design and architecture. The need to know both the meaning of obscure words and the obscure meanings of familiar words is one that a student of any profession encounters early in their studies. In fact the very "putting on of the mantle" of the language of the profession is the very essence of engaging the profession. We find ourselves sounding and thinking like designers and eventually we become the thing we emulate. This list of words will serve as an incomplete but helpful map on this journey.

I, in the process of editing this dictionary encountered many words and illustrations that would extend beyond the scope of any single dictionary. I have also been very involved in the contemporary process of automating the very word management and drawing management tools essential to design practice. I speak of the computer of course. I therefore have combined the extensive database of words and images and the computer and am making available an electronic "encyclopedia" of architecture and design. If you are interested in this product please contact me at 39315 Zacate Avenue, Fremont, CA 94538.

Frederic H. Jones, Ph.D

A

A size sheet: 8 1/2" x 11"

Abacus: The uppermost member of a capital. A plain square slab in the Grecian Doric style, but in other styles often molded or otherwise enriched. Egyptian and Asiatic capitals are often without the abacus.

Abated: In stone cutting, hammered metal work, and the like, cut away or beaten down, lowered in any way, as the background of a piece of ornament, so as to show a pattern or figure in relief.

Abreuvoir: In French, a tank or trough specially for the watering of animals; hardly used in English except for elaborate architectural compositions.

Absolute Coordinates: Coordinates based on points measured from a fixed origin in x, y, or z axes.

Absorption, Sound: Acoustical energy that is converted to heat or another form of energy.

Absorption: (A) Capillary, osmotic, or chemical action by which fibers, yarns, or fabrics become intermixed with liquids or gases. (B) The dissipation of light within a surface or medium.

Abut: To touch, or join, by its end; as in a timber where the end grain is planted against another member of a structure, but without framing; or where an arch bears upon a pier, course of stone, skew back, or the like.

Abutment: A surface of a structure on which a body abuts or presses. Specifically, (A) that which takes the weight and also the thrust of an arch, vault, or truss; usually that part of the wall or pier which may be supposed to be the special support of the construction above. In the case of a series of arches or trusses, the term usually applies to the comparatively heavy piers at the ends and not to the intermediate supports, unless very large. Hence, by extension, but incorrectly, the masonry or rock to which the cables of a suspension bridge are anchored. (B) In carpentry, the joining of two pieces so that their grain is perpendicular.

Abuttal: A piece of ground which bounds on one side the lot or plot under consideration.

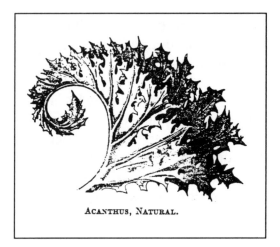

ACANTHUS, NATURAL.

Acanthus: (A) A plant growing freely in the lands of the Mediterranean, having large, deeply cleft leaves; the sharp pointed leaves of some species strongly resembling those of the familiar field and roadside thistles, *Carduus* (or *Cnicus, Gray*) *Lanceolatus, Virginianus*, and others. The two species commonly described and figured, *Acanthus mollis* and *a spinosus*, are very different in the character of the leaves. (B) In Greek, Greco-Roman, Byzantine, Romanesque, and neoclassic architecture, a kind of decorative leafage, assumed to be studied, or to have been studied originally from the plant.

Accent Lighting: Directional lighting to emphasize a particular object or to draw attention to a part of the field of view.

Accessible: A means of approach, admittance, and use for physically handicapped people.

Accolade: An ornamental treatment of the archivolt or hood molding of an arch or of the moldings of an apparent arch, or of a form resembling an arch, as in late Gothic work; consisting of a reverse curve tangent on either side of the curves of the arch or its moldings, and rising to a finial or other ornament above.

Accommodation: The process by which the eye changes focus from one distance to another.

Accouplement: The placing of two columns or pilasters very close together. This device is common in neoclassic church fronts and the like, and is most effective when several pairs of columns form together, a colonnade, as in the celebrated example of the east front of the Louvre. It was almost unknown to Greek or Greco-Roman builders, so far as modern research enables us to say. In the revived classic styles it is considered essential that the capitals should not coalesce; but in medieval work it is common for them to form one block. The placing of a column closely in front of an anta or a pilaster is not considered accouplement.

Acoustic: Used with a basic sound property.

Acoustical Tile: Tiles or sheets that are acoustical absorbents.

Acoustical: Used in the control of sound.

Acoustics: The science of the control and transmission of sound. The unit of measure of sound is the decibel. Zero decibels is no sound. Normal conversation is 45-60 decibels. Hearing injury can occur at more than 100 decibels.

Acrolith: (A) A statue or figure in relief of which only the head, hands, and feet are of stone, the rest being of wood or other material. (B) By extension, such a figure of which the extremities are of finer material than the rest, as of marble applied to inferior stone.

Acropodium: A pedestal for a statue, especially when large and high and adorned with unusual richness. A terminal pedestal or gaine when resting upon representations of the human foot, or even of the feet of animals, is

sometimes specially called acropodium; but the term in this sense is inaccurate and has no classical warrant.

Acropolis: The fortified stronghold or citadel of a Greek city, usually a steep eminence near its center, as at Athens, Corinth, or Tiryns. The shrine of the patron divinity of the city or state was sometimes situated within or upon it, as at Athens. The Athenian Acropolis was, indeed, the artistic as well as the military center of the city and state. Besides the magnificent propylaea by which it was entered, it was adorned with temples and shrines of great beauty, including the Parthenon, Erechtheion, and temple of Nike Apteros. The Acropolis of Corinth was called the Acrocorinthos.

Acroteral, Acroterial: Pertaining to, or having the form of, an acroterium.

Acroteria: Plinths for statues or decoration. They occur at the apex and ends of a pediment.

Acrylic coating cured with radiation process: This material is a coating over particleboard that meets the requirements of the Woodwork Institute of California. The coating meets the requirements of NEMA LQ 1-77, Light Duty and shall be as manufactured by Willamette Industries product known as KorTron/EB.

Adaptation: The process by which the visual system becomes accustomed to more or less light than it was exposed to during an immediately preceding period. It results in a change in the sensitivity of the eye to light.

Admixture: A substance that is added to a mixture of concrete or plaster, usually water repellent, a chemical or color.

Adobe: Sundried mud bricks used for construction in Latin America, Spain, and the American Southwest.

Adytum: The inner sanctuary of a Greek temple. A private sanctuary or chamber.

Aedes: In Roman architecture, any building. A distinction was maintained between *templum*, a regularly consecrated structure or enclosure, and *aedes sacra*, which was a building set apart for pious purposes but not regularly consecrated. In modern inscriptions the term is applied to any public building and is accepted as the equivalent of the English word.

Aedicula: In Roman architecture, a small building; by extension, a shrine set up within a large edifice. Such a shrine may be a mere box or enclosure of wood, or, perhaps, only a screen with pedestal and statue in front of it.

Aedile: A Roman city officer, having special charge of public buildings and streets, and of municipal affairs generally.

Aedility: The government or the care of a city considered with reference to the public buildings, streets, squares, water supply, and other similar functions and duties.

Aerugo: The composition formed upon ancient bronzes by exposure; usually being carbonate of copper, but differing in composition according to the nature of the metal or the soil in which it may have been buried.

Aesymnium: A building erected by or in honor of a person named Aesymnios; especially a tomb in Megara named by Pausanian.

Agger: In Roman building, a large mound or rampart, as of earth. It is applied to the great mound which backs the early wall of Rome, the agger of Servius Tullius, and sometimes to that wall itself, because consisting mainly of an embankment merely faced with dressed stone.

Aggregate: Foreign material like rocks or pebbles mixed with cement to formulate concrete. Exposed aggregate is concrete that contains decorative aggregate that has been processed to expose the aggregate to surface view.

Agiasterium: In the early church, a sanctuary; especially, that part of a basilica in which the altar was set up.

Agnus Dei: A representation in painting or sculpture of the lamb as typical of Christ.

Agora: In Greek archaeology, the market place or open square in a town, nearly corresponding to the Italian Forum. Covered porticoes were built along the sides of the square, in some cases. But little is certain concerning the arrangement of any *agora* of classical Greece.

Agrafe: (A) A cramp or hook used in building; a term used in different senses, but rare. (B) The sculpture in relief put upon the keystone of an arch in ancient Roman and in

neoclassic work. Thus, the archivolt of the Arch of Titus is enriched by an elaborate scroll ornament, upon which is placed a figure almost completely detached from the background.

Aileron: A half gable, such as closes the end of a penthouse roof, or of the aisle of a church. The term signifies, of course, one of two wings. In neoclassic architecture an attempt is frequently made to disguise the actual structure, the sloping roof of the aisle; and the *aileron* takes a nearly independent place as a wing wall shaped like a scroll, as in S. Maria Novella, at Florence; or commonly, like a quarter circle or similar curve, as in S. Zacharia, Venice.

Air Conditioning, Central: A conditioning system that will free the air of humidity and manage the temperature. It will also purify the air.

Air Shaft: A space reserved for the free passage of air, vertically or nearly so; whether small, like an air drain, air duct, or air flue, or forming a small courtyard among high buildings.

Air Space: (A) The space available for the air needed for respiration, as in a sick-room or hospital. Thus it is alleged that the air space in a room is of no avail above twelve feet from the floor; it is said that the air space per person in a barrack room is so many cubic feet. (B) A clear space left between parts of a wall or roof, and intended to exclude dampness; especially between two walls tied together and forming the external wall of a building. Where this precaution is used, furring is not needed.

Air Wood: Wood seasoned by long exposure to the open air, as distinguished from wood which has been dried by artificial heat.

Aisle: (A) In a building whose interior is divided into parts by rows of columns or piers, one of the side divisions, usually lower and smaller than the middle division. In ancient Roman basilicas, Christian basilicas, and the greater number of churches of all epochs, the aisles are straight and parallel, adjoining the nave, the choir, and the higher and chief part of the transept, or such of these divisions as may exist; where, however, the termination of east end, west end, or transept is finished in a rounded apse, the aisle may be continued around the curve. In round churches the aisle is concentric with the nave, and surrounds it. In a few churches there are two aisles on each side of the nave; in a very few, as in the Cathedral of Antwerp, there are three on each side. In many cruciform churches the aisle stops at the transept; in others it returns along one side only, usually the east side, of the transept; in very large churches it sometimes returns on each side, so that a cross section through the transept resembles a similar section across the nave.

In most churches, from the fifth century A.D. to the present time, the roofs of the aisles are lower than the nave roof, etc., so as to allow the direct admission of light through windows pierced in the higher walls above; but in Romanesque churches of central France and on the Rhine the aisles are but little lower than the vaulted nave, etc., from lack of skill on the part of the builders, who needed the resistance of the aisle roofs to the higher vaults; and there is a small class of later churches in which nave and aisles are nearly of the same height. Churches of this class are called Hallenkirchen in Germany, that is, churches resembling halls. Such are the cathedrals (S. Stephen) at Vienna in Austria, Carcassonne in southern France, Erfurt on the Rhine, and the Church of S. Sebaldus in Nurenberg, Bavaria.

The nave vault may be crowned up a little higher than the aisle vault; but there is no clerestory wall with windows. The aisle is usually only one story in height; but in a few Romanesque churches, such as the Cathedral of Tournai in Belgium, and in one or two later ones, such as the Cathedral Notre Dame of Paris, there is an upper story, usually called a gallery, and probably used in the Middle Ages as a place of safe keeping for the property of persons going on a pilgrimage or a crusade. (B) By extension, any one of the longitudinal divisions of an oblong basilica or church; thus, the nave or the higher part of the choir is called the middle aisle, and a church with two aisles on each side is said to be five-aisled. This use of the term is to be longitudinal division. (C) By extension, and, perhaps, by confusion with alley, a walk or passage in a church, or any hall arranged for an audience, giving access to the seats. In this sense wholly popular and modern.

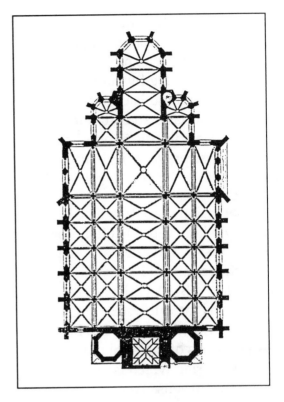

Aisled: Furnished with aisles; most common in combination, forming a term distinguishing the number of aisles, as the Cathedral of Antwerp is seven-aisled. In these cases, the nave is considered as one of the aisles, and the term expresses the number of separate parallel divisions of the structure.

Alabaster: (A) A variety of gypsum; a sulfate of lime more or less translucent and of a prevailing white color, though often clouded and veined with brownish red and other tints. It is soft enough to be readily cut with a knife. A variety brought from Derbyshire in the south of England is used for altar rails in churches and similar decorative adjuncts to buildings, but its softness prevents its being durable.

The Italian variety which is more nearly white, is used chiefly for small vases, statuettes, and the like, which are called "Florentine Marbles." (B) A variety of calcite known as the calcareous or Oriental alabaster, and supposed to be the Alabastrites of the ancient writers. This material, which is much harder than that in sense A, was very largely used in the works of the Romans of antiquity, and quarries in Egypt have been drawn upon in modern times for buildings in Cairo, and even in Europe. The quarries now known, however, would not furnish such large and perfect pieces of hard alabaster as have been found in the ruins of Rome, or as those which stand in the Church of S. Marco in Venice.

Alabastrites: In Roman archaeology, a semiprecious stone, probably the Oriental or calcareous alabaster.

Alameda: In Spain, a promenade, or public garden. These are usually not very large nor of the nature of parks; they are rather alleys or avenues planted with trees and furnished with fountains, seats, grass, and a general covering of gravel, or the like. The formal gardens attached to some towns in the south of France, as Montpelier, should be compared with these.

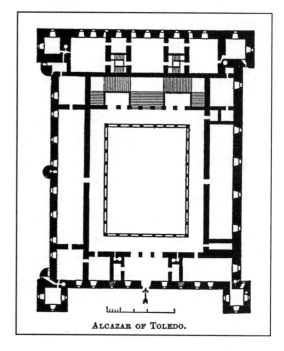

ALCAZAR OF TOLEDO.

Alcazar: In Spain, a palace, generally royal, which is defensible, though not necessarily a strong fortress. The buildings remain from the time of Moorish domination, and often contain much Moorish decoration. The best known examples are those of Segovia, Seville, and Toledo, together with the Alhambra, which is an *alcazar* as well as the others, though not so called in English books.

Alette: In Roman architecture, and in styles derived from this, those parts of a pier which flank the central pilaster or engaged column, and which form the abutments of the arches.

Alhacena: In Spanish architecture, a recess or niche.

Alhambra: A group of buildings on a hill above the city of Granada in southern Spain, forming a fortress palace or *alcazar* of the Moorish kings of Andalusia. The unfinished palace of Charles V adjoins the Moorish buildings. The celebrated decorations of the courts and rooms are partly in ceramic tiles, partly in molded and painted plaster on a wooden framework.

Alinement: The disposing or arranging of anything so that it shall conform to a fixed line or curve; especially a street line. Thus, the arranging of stones in a prehistoric monument, as Stonehenge near Salisbury, or Carnac in Brittany, in determined circles and straight lines, or the placing of houses along a street so that their fronts shall reach and not overpass a fixed limit, are equal instances of alinement. In the case of a city street the alinement may be fixed by law, as where a certain projection of areas and steps upon the sidewalk is allowed, while the house fronts must not pass the line of the property; or it may be fixed by agreement, as where the house fronts of a whole block may be set back a certain number of feet from the property line in order to give wider areas or courtyards in front of the houses. In architectural designing the term is used somewhat vaguely for the employment of long straight lines carefully laid down for the placing of streets and avenues.

Alipterion: An adjoining room in a Roman bath; called also *eloeothesium* and *unctuarium*.

Allee: In French, an alley in the sense of the narrow passage between houses, or under a house; also, an avenue in the sense of a broad walk planted with trees, a promenade, or the like.

Alley: A narrow passage-way; (1) between two houses, like a very narrow street; (2) in or under a house, as affording passage directly to the inner court or yard, without entering the rooms of the house; (3) a walk in a garden; (4) an aisle, as in a church (obsolete); (5) an aisle in the modern sense, that is to say, a passage between the pews, more accurate in this sense than aisle; (6) a long and narrow building.

Almemar: A reading desk in a synagogue; that from which the law is read to the congregation. The term, of Arabic origin, is in use in the Jewish worship in many countries. In Spain and Portugal the same reading desk is called *Tebah*.

Almena: The curiously indented and generally trapezoidal battlement used in some buildings of the south and east of Europe; a Spanish term, probably of Arabic derivation. The Spanish word signifies also a turret or small tower, perhaps also a pinnacle, which uses do not seem to have been followed in English.

Almonry: A place, sometimes a separate house, where the alms of a great abbey, city or a magnate were distributed.

Alms Gate: In an abbey or manor house the gate in the bounding wall or courtyard wall where alms were distributed.

Altar-tomb: A tomb resembling an altar but not used for one.

Altar: A table or structure used in religious places and rites to hold a sacrifice or offering to a deity.

Ambo: A Bible stand used in a Christian church for the reading of the Gospel and Epistle.

Amphiprostyle: A temple with porticoes at each end and no columns at the sides.

Amphitheater: A circular sports, exhibition, or theatrical space enclosed by tiers of seats. In ancient times the site of gladiatorial contests.

Anathyrosis: A smooth dressing of the outer contact band of a masonry joint.

Ancones: Projections left on blocks of stone or carvings used to lift them into position. Brackets beside a doorway that support a cornice.

Angular Capital: An Ionic capital with the volutes turned outward and all four sides alike.

Anta: In classical architecture a pilaster which does not conform to the primary order of the building.

Antechurch: An addition to the west end of a church. It usually resembles a narthex or porch.

Antefixae: Ornamental blocks used to conceal the ends of tiles on the edge of a roof.

Antependium: A cloth or metal altar covering that hangs over the front edge.

Anthemion: Classical ornament based on honeysuckle flowers and leaves.

Anticlastic: A surface with curvatures both concave and convex through any point. A hyperbolic parabolic roof is an example.

Apex Stone: The top stone in a gable end. Also called a saddle stone.

Apophyge: A curve that occurs at the top and bottom of a column where the shaft joins the base or capital.

Apron: A raised panel below a window sill. An addition or

extension to the front of a stage platform.

APSE: ENGLISH, 13TH CENTURY; TIDMARSH, BERKSHIRE.

Apse: A polygonal or semicircular vault, often occurring in a chapel or chancel.

Apteral: A classical building with the columns at the ends rather than the sides.

Aqueduct: A channel constructed to carry water. It is often elevated.

Aquinch: An arch, lintel, corbelling, or system of such members, built across the interior corner of two walls, as at the top of a tower, to serve as foundation for the diagonal or canted side of a superimposed octagonal spire or lantern. The squinch performs the functions of a pendentive.

Araeostyle: An arrangement of columns spaced four diameters apart.

Arcade, Surface: An arcade or system of arches built against the surface of a wall, or partially or wholly imbedded in it, generally for decoration, as frequently in Romanesque and medieval architecture; a blind arcade; called also Wall Arcade.

INTERSECTING ARCADE: CHRIST CHURCH, OXFORD; CLOSE OF 12TH CENTURY.

Arcade: (A) Two or more arches with their imposts, piers, columns, or the like taken together and considered as a single architectural feature. It is more common to use the term for a considerable number of arches, and especially where they are small and where the whole feature is as much decorative as useful. Thus, one of the four sides of a vaulted cloister would be more commonly spoken of as an ambulatory or a gallery, although the word arcade might be used for the row of arches as they are seen from the garth within.

The arcade is a favorite decorative feature in nearly all arcuated styles and especially in those of the Middle Ages. Thus, in the front of a Gothic cathedral there is very commonly a large arcade raised high above the portals and having each of its arches filled with a statue. In the well-known front of Notre Dame in Paris an arcade of twenty-nine arches comes immediately above the great doorways. Each of these arches is filled with a statue of a king or a queen, and the whole is known as the Royal Gallery, a term used in connection with other churches as well. High up in the front, above the great rosewindow, is a second arcade of four great double arches to each tower and four similar ones between the towers; these last open and show the peak of the roof beyond, while minor arches adorn the buttresses. This second arcade is on a great scale, the larger arches having about 8 feet span and rising 24 feet above the bases of their columns, while yet the arcade is purely ornamental, except in so far as it covers a narrow gallery for the caretakers or workmen.

Similar arcades are used in the interior of Gothic churches and very commonly in English architecture. It is certainly a more dignified and worthy system of design when these arcades can be used to stiffen the walls which they adorn, and to a certain extent this is done in the Romanesque and Gothic work; still, however, the arcade is usually a purely decorative feature. (B) A single arched opening, with its abutment, etc.; rare in this usage, which is borrowed from the French; but occurring in carefully written matter, as when a Roman memorial arch is spoken of as having one, two, or three "arcades." (C) In English, and forming part of a proper name, a covered gallery with shops or booths along its side. The Lowther Arcade and Burlington Arcade are well-known buildings of this sort in London. A very large building of this sort exists in Moscow, having been erected in the seventeenth century; in this there is an upper balcony connecting with several bridges which cross the open space; and a second row of shops opens upon this balcony. There is no English name for this kind of structure, which is the nearest European approach to the oriental bazaar. Enterprises of the sort are not common, and neither in French, Italian, nor English is there a special name for them.

Arcade, Intersecting: In the Romanesque architecture of the north, one whose archivolts cross one another, being curved in imitation of interlacing bands. Many instances of this curious decoration exist in England; it is naturally limited to purely decorative arcades not large in scale nor deeply recessed.

Arch, Abutment: That arch of a series which comes next to the outer abutment; as the land arch of a bridge.

Arch, Back: An arch carrying the back or inner part of a wall, where the exterior face of the wall is carried in a different way; as above a window opening, which has a stone lintel for the outer part of the wall and a concealed arch carrying the inner part.

Arch, Basket Handle: A three-centered arch of the more usual kind. The term might equally well be applied to a five-centered or seven-centered arch having the same general form.

BELL ARCH.
From a belfry in a Swiss village above Vevay.

Arch, Bell: An arch resting upon two corbels with curved face or

edge, so that the resulting compound curve has a distant resemblance to the outlines of a bell.

Arch, Built: One composed of material other then masonry and put together with rivets, spikes, or the like; therefore not depending upon the mutual support of voussoirs, nor yet a solid ring of masonry. The simplest form is the laminated arch. The more elaborate forms are more usually called by such names as arched truss or arch truss, and instances of this latter class are to be seen in such great interiors as the Grand Central railway station at New York, and in bridges such as the Washington Bridge across the Harlem River, New York City.

Arch, Camber: Same as Flat Arch; so called because it is usual to give to the intrados, and sometimes to the extrados as well, a very slight camber. It is, of course, an arch with a scarcely perceptible segmental curve.

Arch, Catenarian: An arch whose intrados or central line is a catenary curve; extremely rare in architecture, though not uncommon in engineering.

CHANCEL ARCH, HEADINGTON, OXFORDSHIRE; MIDDLE 12TH CENTURY.

Arch, Chancel: The arch at the west end of a chancel.

Arch, Compound: Same as Built Arch.

Arch, Contrasted: An Ogee Arch, or one with a reverse curve.

Arch, Cusp: One which has cusps or foliations worked on the intrados.

Arch, Cycloidal: One whose intrados or center line is a cycloid; a form thought to have been recognized in the architecture of India.

Arch, Depressed: Same as Drop Arch.

Arch, Diaphragm: A transverse arch across the nave of a church.

Arch, Diminished: An arch having less rise or height than a semicircle; whether segmental, multi-centered, or elliptical. The term is not in common use.

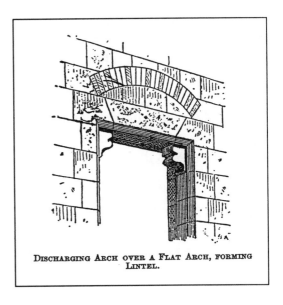

DISCHARGING ARCH OVER A FLAT ARCH, FORMING LINTEL.

Arch, Discharging: One built over a lintel or similar closure or opening in a wall, and intended as an appliance for throwing the load above an opening to the piers on both sides and thus relieving the lintel or flat arch from the danger of being fractured or dislocated. In the case of an arched doorway, where there is a tympanum under the arch or a lintel with a glazed light above it, the arch is considered as the principal thing, and the lintel, or as it is sometimes called, the transom, as an accessory; and here the term "discharging arch" would hardly be used. In some cases the discharging piece, of whatever nature, is concealed. Thus, in Roman and neoclassic buildings the architrave may be composed of voussoirs, and this flat arch may be relieved by a discharging arch, above each intercolumniation, and this may occupy the whole height of the frieze, which thus masks or even wholly conceals the discharging arch.

Arch, Drop: (A) A pointed arch in which the two centers are nearer together than the width of the arch, so that the radii are less than the span. (B) One in which the centers or some of the centers are below the springing line, as in Basket Handle Arch.

Arch, Equilateral Pointed: See Pointed Arch.

Arch, Extradosed: One which has the extrados clearly marked, as a curve exactly or nearly parallel to

the intrados, therein differing from an arch whose voussoirs are cut with horizontal returns so as to pass into the masonry of the wall. The extradosed arch has then a well-marked archivolt.

Arch, Flat: One having a horizontal or nearly horizontal intrados, and, in most cases, a horizontal extrados as well. A flat arch with slightly concave intrados is called a Camber Arch. When built of brick the radiation of the voussoirs is effected in cheap work by the thickening of the joints outward; in finer work, by cutting or rubbing the brick to the required taper, or by the use of specially molded bricks. Such arches are for square-headed openings and in fireproof flooring between steel or iron beams. Their transverse weakness and great thrust make them undesirable for heavy structural work, and in walls they are consequently often relieved by discharging arches. Fireproof floor arches are built of specially designed hollow voussoirs burned very hard, and capable of sustaining a heavy load up to seven or eight feet span.

Flat arches occur in Roman work both in brick and stone, relieved as above mentioned by discharging arches. A similar construction is much more common in Arabic buildings and to some extent in Turkish, being made a decorative feature, constructed with alternate voussoirs of dark and white marble ingeniously toggled together by cutting the cheeks into interlocking patterns, and pushing the voussoirs in from the front. In some cases this is a mere veneering, covering brickwork or rubble. Somewhat similar flat arches occur in the hoods and openings of some medieval fireplaces. In Lincoln Cathedral there is a stone arch, nearly flat, of over 30 feet span between the two towers of the front; but such examples are very rare.

The strongly projecting architraves over engaged columns, both in Roman and modern work, are often of several pieces cut to form a flat arch, and this is true even of architraves over free columns when these are too widely spaced for safety with monolithic architraves; but in modern architecture such joints are commonly cut merely for the appearance of stability, a concealed metal beam really sustaining the flat arch and its load.

Arch, Foiled: Same as Cusped Arch.

Arch, Groin: See also Vault, Groin.

Arch, Hand: One turned without centering, usually by the aid of a board whose edge is cut to the required curve, and serving as a template.

Arch, Hanse; Haunch Arch; Haunched Arch: One of which the crown is of different curve from the haunches, which are thus strongly marked; usually a Basket Handle or three-centered or four-centered arch.

Arch, Horseshoe: One in which the curves are carried below the springing line so that the opening at the bottom of the arch is less than its greatest span; see the general article above.

Arch, Imperfect: All these terms seem to arise in the natural to academic students of neo-Russian style, that all arches not semicircular are in some way incorrect.

Arch, Inflected: Same as Inverted Arch.

Arch, Inverted: One whose springing lines is above the intrados and the intrados above the extrados. Such arches are used in construction, as in foundations where very narrow piers have to be given a wider bearing upon the soil. The conditions are almost precisely similar to those of arches resting upon piers and with a superincumbent mass. In lofty modern buildings inverted arches are not common, as engineers prefer to give to each pier an unyielding and inelastic support.

Arch, Jack: Same as Flat Arch; also any arch doing rough work, or slightly or roughly built.

Arch, Laminated: One built of thin pieces of material, such as boards, which are successively bent to the curve, each around the one below, and finally bolted or spiked together. Such pieces are laid so as to break joints and may be used 10 or 20 thick in a single laminated arch.

LANCET ARCH, WESTMINSTER ABBEY.

Arch, Lancet: A pointed arch whose centers are farther apart than the width or span of the arch.

Arch, Land: In a bridge or viaduct crossing a stream or valley, one of the two arches which come next to the bank and which spring from the exterior abutment.

Arch, Lobed: Same as Cusped Arch.

Arch, Moorish: Same as Horseshoe Arch.

Arch, Oblique: Same as Skew Arch. The term is also applied, but improperly, to a Rampant Arch.

Arch, Ogee: One having a reverse curve at the point. The name is most often applied to an arch which has only two centers on the springing line (in this, like an ordinary pointed arch) and two centers for the reversed curve; but many ogee arches have four centers for the arch proper and two for the reverse curve.

Arch, Ogival: A pointed arch of the type most common in Gothic architecture; a mistaken use of the French term.

Arch, Pointed: One in which two curves meet at the crown at an angle, more or less acute. Ordinary two-centered pointed arches are called lancet or acute, equilateral, and blunt. Some Italian arches are of unusual form, with extrados and intrados not concentric. The pointed form is, like the round form, of unknown antiquity. Perhaps the earliest use of it as an important part of an architectural style is to be found in mosques, such as that of Tulun in Cairo (though it is asserted that the Coptic builders in Egypt used it from an earlier time). It was used in Romanesque work in the West, though never very freely. When, therefore, the system of rib vaulting was in the earliest stages of its development, the pointed arch was ready at hand, a familiar expedient; and its utility under the new conditions became evident. Adopted thus as a necessary part of the construction, it became also the characteristic decorative feature of the new style. Acute, blunt, and equilateral arches were freely used in the same building; but the four-centered arches were not used until a very late time. The two-centered segmental arch was a still later piece of decadence.

Arch, Raking: Same as Rampant Arch.

Arch, Rampant: One in which the impost on one side is higher than that on the other. Thus, in a stone balustrade for a staircase, the small arches supporting the hand rail spring upward from the top of one baluster to the top of another. The curve may be of any shape which allows of imposts being placed continually higher from one end to the other of the arcade.

Arch, Rear: An arch spanning a window opening or doorway inside a wall.

Arch, Relieving: Same as Discharging Arch.

Arch, Rollock or Row-Lock: One in which the bricks or other very small pieces of solid material are arranged in separate concentric rings. Such arches are common in simple brick masonry.

Arch, Round: One of semicircular curve; usually limited to one which is very slightly stilted, if at all, so that its appearance is of a semicircle and of no more, above the imposts. This form is the only one used in Roman Imperial, Byzantine, Romanesque, and cognate styles, as well as much the most common form in Renaissance and Post-Renaissance architecture. These are often classed together, roughly, as the round-arched styles.

Arch, Safety: A discharging arch; an arch thrown over a lintel to relieve it, or under a bearing to distribute it over a larger surface of wall.

Arch, Scheme: Same as Diminished Arch. The term seems to be derived from the Italian *scemo*, "diminished" or "lowered." Spelled also Skeen.

Arch, Segment Arch; Segmental Arch: One having for the curve of its intrados and extrados concentric segments of circles and whose center, therefore, is a certain distance below the angle made by the impost with the inner face of the abutment, such as the jamb of a door or window.

Arch, Skew: One in which the archivolt on either side is in a plane not at right angles with the face of the abutment. Thus, if a doorway is carried through a thick wall in a direction not at right angles with the face of that wall, the arched head of that doorway would be called a skew arch, being really a barrel vault whose axis is at an oblique angle with the face of the wall.

Arch, Splayed: An arch opening which has a larger radius at one side than at the other. As was said above of the skew arch, this is a vault rather than an arch proper. An accurate term for it would be conical vault.

Arch, Stilted: One in which the architectural impost, with its moldings, abacus, string-course, or the like is notably lower than the springing line; so that the intrados passes into the vertical jamb of the opening, and this is continued downward as if a part of the intrados. The whole archivolt follows this form.

Arch, Straight: Same as Flat Arch.

Arch, Straining: An arch used as a strut, as in a flying buttress.

Arch, Surbased: A depressed arch; an arch of which the rise is less than half the span.

Arch, Surmounted: A stilted semicircular arch; a semicircular arch of which the center is above the impost.

Arch, Three-lobed: One of which each haunch is developed into a cusplike form; so that the archivolt itself, if there is one plainly distinguished, or the intrados alone, assumes the form of a trefoil. The form with a complete archivolt is rare, but occurs on a large scale in the Cathedral of Tournai. The form where the intrados only is three-lobed occurs in many arcades, usually small, of the thirteenth century.

Arch, Transverse: The arched construction built across a hall, the nave of a church, or the like, either as part of the vaulting or to support or stiffen the roof in some other way, or to furnish a solid substructure for the centering. In Romanesque vaulting, the transverse arch is hardly of use, except as an assistant in fixing the centering, but the timid

builders of the time preserved it as a possible needed aid, especially in the building of groined vaults. In Gothic vaulting it is the rib which crosses the nave, aisle, or the like, and divides the vaulting into compartments. Where there is no vaulting, an arch is sometimes built across the interior, carrying a wall which supports the purlins and other longitudinal timbers of the roof.

Arch, Triangular: (A) The corbel arch of the Maya. (B) A structure composed of two stones supporting one another mutually so as to span an opening.

Arch, Trimmer: An arch, usually of brickwork and of very low rise, built between the trimmers where a floor is framed around a chimney breast. Its thrust is taken up usually by the stiffness of the header on the one side and by the brickwork of the chimney breast on the other. Its purpose is to support the hearth of the fireplace in the story above.

Arch, Tudor: A four-centered pointed arch so called because common in the architecture of the Tudor style in England.

Arch Braces: A pair of curved braces forming an arch.

Arch: (A) A structural member rounded vertically to span an opening or recess; in this sense the term is used either for a decorative or memoria building, of which an upward curving member forms the principal feature and spans a gate or passage below, or for the member itself, considered as a firm and resistant curved bar capable of bearing weight and pressure. In this, the original sense, a wicker device thrown across a street or passage and covered with foliage and flowers, is as much an arch as a more permanent structure. (B) A mechanical means of spanning an opening by heavy wedge-shaped solids which mutually keep one another in place, and which transform the vertical pressure of the superincumbent load into two lateral components transmitted to the abutments. The shape is indifferent, although arches are generally curved. The width or thickness, horizontally, is also indifferent, although an arch which acts as a roof and covers much horizontal space is called a vault.

The constructional arch has been known from great antiquity, but it was rarely used by the ancients except for drains or similar underground and hidden conveniences. It appears, however, that the Assyrian builders used it freely as a means of roofing their long and narrow palace walls. Assyrian vaults were built of unbaked brick put together with mortar, so that the anchor vault became a continuous and massive shell. On the other hand, the Etruscans from a very early time understood the principle of the arch so well that they built arches of cut stone in large separate voussoirs put together without mortar. For us, the Etruscans were the originators of the true self-supporting arch. It was adopted from them by the Romans; but both these nations confined themselves almost exclusively to the semicircular arch, both in spanning openings in walls and for purposes of vaulting.

The pointed arch seems to have been known as early as the round arch. It is, indeed, an obvious way of making an arch which shall have greater height in proportion to its width, and which shall in this way be stronger, because having less outward thrust. Its use in pre-Gothic, as in early Islamic architecture, and in Romanesque buildings, as in S. Front at Perigueus, is merely occasional and because of some preference on the part of the individual builder.

The three-centered arch and the four-centered arch are both much used in the transitional work of the sixteenth century in Northern Europe. The segmental arch has hardly been used for decorative purposes, except occasionally in the Louis Quatorze style, before the present half century; it is now rather common in French work, and it may be that more could be made of it, architecturally speaking, than in the past.

The flat arch is used commonly to produce a similitude of trabeated construction when in reality the stones accessible are too small for the great spans required. Thus, in Roman and neoclassic buildings, the epistyle or architrave between two columns is often made of separate voussoirs in this way, as in the Pantheon of Paris.

Mechanically, an arch may be considered as any piece or assemblage of pieces so arranged over an opening that the vertical pressure of the supported load is transformed into two lateral inclined pressures on the abutments.

ARCH: TRANSVERSE ARCH.

Considered in this light, then, the stone window head shown in (Fig. 1) is truly an arch. The stone is wedge-shaped; and it will be readily seen that the load on it has a tendency to force this wedge down into the window opening by pushing the adjoining masonry away to the right and left, as shown by the arrows.

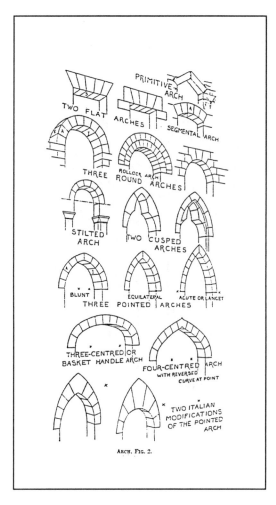

TWO FLAT ARCHES

PRIMITIVE ARCH

SEGMENTAL ARCH

THREE ROUND ARCHES

ROLLOCK ARCH

STILTED ARCH

TWO CUSPED ARCHES

BLUNT
THREE

EQUILATERAL
POINTED

ACUTE OR LANCET
ARCHES

THREE-CENTRED OR
BASKET HANDLE ARCH

FOUR-CENTRED ARCH
WITH REVERSED
CURVE AT POINT

TWO ITALIAN
MODIFICATIONS
OF THE POINTED
ARCH

ARCH. FIG. 2.

and its function fulfilled by a weight at the feet of the rafters.

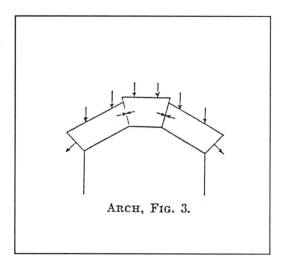

ARCH, FIG. 3.

An arch slightly more elaborate is the primitive arch shown in Fig. 2. Here two wedge-shaped stones lean against each other, and each one transmits pressures similar to those just described, the pressures at the respective upper ends counteracting each other. This form of arch may be compared to a pair of rafters whose tiebeam has been removed

To go a step farther, we have an arch made of three stones, as shown in Fig. 3, each one of which is acting as an independent wedge tending to force its way inward, and so exerting a lateral pressure at each of its oblique ends, while the combination of all these six pressures results in a lateral push on each abutment as shown by the arrows. This lateral push, in Figs. 2 and 3, is similar to that in Fig. 1, from which it differs in direction, owing to the inclination of the end pieces; were these more steeply inclined they would evidently exert a push more nearly vertical. Hence, the higher the arch in proportion to its span, the less lateral push will it exert. The foregoing considerations will be found to apply equally well to all of the arches shown in Fig. 2, or to any other similar construction of wedge-shaped pieces. It will also be observed that, in the case of two or more such wedges, each one is being acted upon by the adjoining pieces, which tend to force it outward; this tendency is overcome only by proper and more or less uniform distribution of the loads to be carried. The lateral pressure on the abutment is known as the thrust, and resistance to this force was the subject of constant experiment in the church building of the Middle Ages, resulting in the elaborate systems of engaged and flying buttresses. Arches may be divided according to their form into the following classes:--(1) The Flat Arch; (2) The arch with one center; (a) semicircular or Round Arch; (b) Segmental Arch; (c) Horseshoe Arch. (3) With two centers; (a) Equilateral Pointed Arch; (b) Lancet Arch; (c) Drop Arch or Blunt Pointed Arch; (d) Pointed Horseshoe Arch; (e) Drop Arch in the second sense. These five varieties are what is known as pointed arches; the first three being those in use in many styles. (4) With three centers; (a) Basket Handle Arch; (b) the round arch with

reversed curve at crown. (5) With four centers; (a) that form of pointed arch in which two of the centers are on the springing line and two below; (b) that in which a two-centered arch is prolonged at top with a reversed curve (see Ogee Arch). It is evident that a six-centered arch might be composed by giving to the form (6) (a) a reversed curve as in the other instances; but such subdivisions may be continued indefinitely; thus a five-centered arch might be developed out of the basket handle arch; and so on. An arch is divisible into the haunches, or reins, and the crown. An arch is made up of *voussoirs*, of which there may be one in the middle occupying the center of the crown and called a kaystone. The inner side of the arch ring is called the intrados. The outer side of the arch ring is called the extrados, or back. When an arch is laid down on paper the horizontal line which passes through the center in the plane of the arch, if there is but one, or which connects two centers, and which (except in the segmental arches, one- or two-centered) marks the place at which the curve of the arch joins the vertical line of the abutment, is called the springing line. The height from the springing line to the intrados (or to the line which in a drawing represents the intrados) is the height or rise; sometimes called the versed line. The width between the two points of juncture above mentioned is the span. That part of an arch which forms a part of the face of the wall is called the face of the arch, or very commonly, the archivolt. Parts of the construction immediately dependent upon or connected with an arch are the abutment; impost; skew back; spandrel; springer.

Archaic: Pertaining to or having the character of extremely early and primitive work. As applied to different branches of art, the term refers to different but specific periods; as, for example, in Greek art, to the formative period between the Heroic or Homeric Age, and the middle or end of the sixth century B.C. Archaic is distinguished from primitive art by its evidence of those definite progressive tendencies which give form to the later and more perfect art.

Architect: A person who designs, draws plans, and manages the construction of a building.

Architectural Terra Cotta: Clay that is burned and used in building units.

Architectural: (A) Pertaining to architecture; as, an architectural publication or drawing. (B) Having the character of a work of architecture; as, an architectural composition. (C) Composed or treated in accordance with the principles of architecture; as, an architectural decoration.

Architrave: A molded frame surrounding a window or door. The lowest part of an entablature.

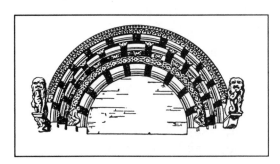

Archivolt: A continuous architrave molding on the face of an arch.

Arcuated: A building structurally dependent on arches, in contrast to a trabeated building.

Arena: The open space of an amphitheater. A building primarily used for sports and exhibitions.

Ashlar, Bastard: Stone in thin blocks or slabs which is used to face walls of brick or rubble, and so treated as to resemble solid blocks of stone. This material is often set edgeways, or with natural bed nearly vertical.

Ashlar, Broken: That in which the stones are of different sizes and shapes, though always rectangular on the face.

Ashlar, Coursed: That in which the stones are arranged according to height, so as to form regular courses in the face of the wall.

Ashlar, Random Coursed: That formed by squared stones of various and irregular sizes, but laid so as to form high courses, each of which is laid as a band of broken ashlar.

Ashlar, Random Range: Same as Broken Ashlar.

Ashlar, Rough: Rough stone, little or not at all dressed after quarrying.

Ashlar Masonry: Rectangular units of burned clay used in masonry.

Ashlar Pece: A roof element consisting of a short vertical timber connecting an inner wall plate to a rafter above.

Ashlar; Ashler: Masonry blocks hewn with even faces and square edges and laid in horizontal courses with vertical joints. This is in contrast to rubble or unhewn stone. (A) Squared and finished building stone; in recent times, especially, such stone when used for the face of a wall whose substance is made of inferior material. The term has usually a general signification, and a single piece would be called a block of ashlar; rarely, an ashlar. An attempt has been made to limit the term to stone which is set on its edge, that is to say, not on the quarry bed, and in this way to serve as a translation of the French adjectival phrase *en delit*; but there seems to be no authority for this limitation. (B) Attributively, and in combination, having the appearance of, or to be used in the place of, ashlar, as a veneer. (C) A vertical stud between the sloping roof and flooring in a garret or roof story, by a series of which vertical walls are provided for the sides of rooms, and the angular space near the eaves partitioned off either as waste space or as low closets.

Atelier: A workshop or studio; the French term naturalized in English for an artist's studio, and, especially, for one of those studios in which pupils are trained in any fine art.

Atrium: The inner open court of a building surrounded on multiple sides by the building or roof, often occurring in residential structures. A colonnaded quadrangle in medieval church architecture.

Attic Base: Base of an Greek ionic column. It consists of two large rings of convex molding joined by a spreading concave molding.

Attic Story: A room or upper story in a building or house often directly under the roof. In classical architecture, a story above the main entablature of a building.

Attribute: An object, as a weapon, a flower, or the like, considered as expressing the character or authority of a divinity; thus the dove is a recognized attribute of Venus in Roman and modern mythology.

Aumbry: A storage space or cupboard used to store ritual vessels in a church.

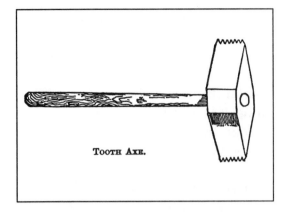

TOOTH AXE.

Axe, Tooth: Axe with the edges having teeth, used in finishing the face of the softer kinds of stones or in preparing them for a still finer finish.

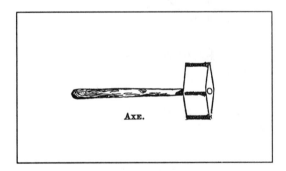

AXE.

Axe: (A) In French, the axis; the central or determining line. *En Axe.* In French, placed upon the axis, as of something else; or symmetrically disposed about the axis. A monument is said to be *en axe* with a street when the center line of the street passes through the center of the monument. Two rooms are said to be *en axe*, or an opposite window or door, or two opposite doors, are said to be *en axe* when the axis of the room, pavilion, wing, or whole building passes through them, or even when they are centered upon one another with deliberate care to bring them exactly opposite. The term, being entirely French, is taken over into English with many abuses and misunderstandings. (B): A form of peen hammer used for the rougher kinds of stone dressing. Its head has the form of a double wedge with its two edges parallel to the handle.

Axial Plan: A building planned along an axis or longitudinally.

Axial: (A) Pertaining to an axis, as in the expression, an axial line. (B) Situated on an axis, as any member of a building, either existing or shown in a drawing. The term is not common in architectural writing, but occurs sometimes as a substitute for *en axe* and to avoid circumlocution.

Axis: (A) In architectural drawing, a central line, not necessarily intended to form a part of the finished drawing, but laid down as a guiding line from which may be measured figure dimensions of

rooms, the widths of openings, etc. A primary axis may pass through the middle of the ground plan. There may be as many subsidiary axes as the different rooms, wings, pavilions, or other primary parts of the building may require. (B) An imaginary line to which is referred the parts of an existing building or the relations of a number of buildings to one another. Thus, in Greek architecture, the buildings standing on the Acropolis of Athens, or those within the sacred enclosure at Epidauros or Olympia, have each a distinctly marked axis, but have no common axis that modern explorers have been able to fix. Such buildings are, indeed, set at angles with one another so obvious that the idea of a common axis is precluded. On the other hand, the great temple at Karnak in Egypt has a bent or deviated axis; that is to say, while the first three or four halls and courts have evidently been carefully arranged upon one axis, those that follow are arranged upon another axis, making a very slight angle with the former one. A similar deflection occurs in many medieval churches, and a legend exists, very hard to verify, according to which this change of direction from the nave to the choir is intended to suggest the reclining of the Saviour's head upon the cross. All careful planning is done with some reference to an axis, but the designers of different schools disagree widely as to the value to be given to the placing of buildings and parts of buildings accurately upon an axis, or as it is called, following the French term, *En Axe.* (C) One of three perpendicular lines intersecting at a common point in space.

Axminster Carpet: One of the basic weaves that originated in the 1700's in the town of Axminster, England.

Axminster Weave: A woven carpet type. Unlike the Wilton weave, almost all the pile yarns appear on the surface of Axminster carpeting. The pile tufts are anchored by stiff weft shots of jute, kraftcord, or synthetic fibers running across the width of the carpet. The surface yarns are usually cut and of one height woven into geometric and floral patterns in an almost limitless variety of designs and colors.

Axonometric Projection: A drawing showing an object or building in three dimensions. The plan is organized at an appropriate angle and all dimensions on both the horizontal and vertical plane are to scale. Diagonals and curves on the vertical plane are distorted.

Azulejos: Glazed pottery tiles used in Spanish and Latin American buildings. They are usually painted with bright colors and floral and exaggerated decorative patterns.

B

Back: (A) The more remote or further side of any member or part of a building, or what may have seemed more remote to the designer. (B) The rear of a building, in any sense. Where both of the longer faces of a large building are treated with nearly equal architectural effect, that face which has not the principal entrance will be the back. Churches, while they often have a front, can hardly be said to have a back, because the chancel end, commonly called the east end, is peculiarly important in the ecclesiological sense, and frequently has exceptionally important architectural features. In the plural, as "the backs," that side of a long row of buildings which is opposite their principal fronts, as in Cambridge University (England), where the term covers the buildings as seen from the river. (C) The top or upper surface or portion of a member, as the back of a hand rail; the back of an arch, meaning the extrados. (D) In composition, the reverse or inner side; a lining or the like.

Bailey: The open court of a stone castle. Also called a ward.

Balance: Equal value of weight on the right and left sides of a room.

Balcony: A platform projecting from wall, door or a window sill and enclosed with a railing. It may be cantilevered or supported by brackets or columns.

Baldachin; Baldaquin: (A) A canopy made of a textile fabric (originally of baudekyn; a precious stuff brought from Baldacca or Bagdad), used in processions, placed over an episcopal chair and throne of state, or suspended over an altar where there is no ciborium. (B) A permanent canopy, especially above the high altar of a church; in this sense applied to the most massive and permanent structures, as the bronze baldachin in S. Peter's at Rome which is stated to be 95 feet high.

Balistraria: Cross-shaped openings in medieval military battlements used to fire bows while affording protection.

Balk: (A) A heavy piece of timber, of any kind not in the log. A squared timber. (B) By extension from the above meaning, in primitive country houses of Great Britain, a loft formed by sawing planks or poles on the balks or main timbers of the framing. Commonly in the plural.

Baluster: A short colonette usually complete with shaft, cap, and base, and used as one of many to support the hand rail or horizontal top member of a low screen or parapet. In modern times the term is applied to the similar member which forms one of the comparatively slight, vertical supports of a hand rail of the ordinary type.

Balustrade: A short series of pillars or balusters terminated on top with a rail.

BARGEBOARD AT SHREWSBURY, SHROPSHIRE; ABOUT 1350 (THE WINDOW IS LATER).

Bargeboards: Boards placed against the incline of a building or gable to hide the horizontal rafters or beams.

Base Block: A block of any material, generally with little or no ornament, forming the lowest member of a base, or itself fulfilling the functions of a base; specifically, a member sometimes applied to the foot of a door or window trim.

Base Line: (A) In architectural drawings, the lowest horizontal line; the line which marks the base or bottom of the design; especially, in perspective, the trace of the picture plane on the ground plane. (B) In engineering and surveying, the first line determined upon, located, and measured as a base from which other lines, angles, and distances are laid out or computed in surveying or plotting a piece of ground for a map or plan.

Base-shoe: Molding applied to a wall where it meets the floor in order to prevent damage.

BASE OF IONIC ORDER; THE ERECHTHEUM, ATHENS.

Base: The lowest part or the lowest main division of anything, as of a column, pier, the front of a building or of a pavilion, tower, or the like. The term is used independently in the following senses:--(A) The lowest of the three principal parts of a column, when the column is so divided. Many Egyptian columns and the columns of the Grecian Doric order have no bases; moreover, in other styles many pillars, which, from their

approximately cylindrical form are called columns, have no base in the strict sense here given to the term. The traditional base of the Ionic columns of one of the porches of the Erechtheum in Athens is made of, first, a group of hollow moldings divided by narrow fillets, below this a larger cove between two fillets, and below this a convex molding almost semicylindrical in section, called generally a Torus. The Attic base, so called, consists of the following members, beginning at the top: a convex molding of nearly semicylindrical section; a scotia between two fillets; another convex molding somewhat larger than the upper one. The base of the medieval columns, Eastern and Western, Byzantine, Romanesque, and Gothic, are extraordinarily varied, and it is evident that the artist tried many combinations of moldings, retaining for frequent use only those which were the most agreeable to the eye and expressive of the function of the base, which is, of course, to extend somewhat the area of pressure. As the use of the square plinth below the base had been adopted from Roman practice, and had become very common, the medieval builders adopted a spur to fill each of the four corners of this plinth and to extend still more the even pressure of the base upon the plinth. (B) The lowest part of a wall or pier, especially if ornamented by moldings or by a projecting feature decorated by panelling or sculpture. In this sense the term is incapable of accurate and exhaustive definition, as the lowermost course of stone in the exterior of a wall, where it shows above the pavement or the surface of the ground, is capable of an infinite variety of artistic treatments. Hence,--(C) A member of any material applied as a finish or protection at the foot of a wall, or the like, especially in interior finish, as a baseboard forming part of the wooden trim of a room.

Basement: (A) The lower part of the wall or walls of any building, especially when divided from the upper porticoes in an architectural way, as by a different material, a different and perhaps more solid architectural treatment, smaller and fewer windows, or the like. The basement may occupy only a small part of the whole height of the structure, or it may be even more than half of that height, as in some palaces of the Italian Renaissance, especially in North Italy. It frequently happens that there is a double basement; that is to say, the basement proper, serving as a foil and a support to the more elaborate story or stories above, has itself a still more massive basement, probably without openings. (B) The story which comes, in the construction of the building, behind the piece of wall above described; in this sense, an abbreviation of the term "basement story." Originally, this story would have its floor almost exactly on a level with the street without, or with the courtyard; but in some buildings it is raised several steps above the street, and in others its floor is some distance below the street, as, notably, in city dwelling houses.

Basilica: A church with a nave and two or more aisles. The nave is higher and wider than the aisles. In classical architecture it refers to a large meeting hall.

Bastion: A projection at the angle of a fortification.

Batten Plates: Tie plates at the ends of compression members, or used at intervals to connect the channel beams of Z beams, which form the column or strut, replacing, for instance, the latticing on the open side or a built strut of column.

Batten: A piece of wood that covers the connecting parts of boards or panels. In English usage, a plank of 7" x 2 1/2"or 7" x 3", which may be cut into three boards or deals. The term is also applied to furring strips for flooring or plastering. In American usage, any thin and narrow strip of wood such as may be used for nailing over the joints between the boards of the siding of framed houses.

Battening: The affixing of battens to a wall or frame; or the whole system of battens so affixed. In English usage, the application of furring strips to a wall or roof frame for plastering, or to joists to receive the flooring. This is usually called furring in the United States.

Bay: (A) An opening, as of a window or door, or as between two columns or piers. In this sense, the French *baie* should be consulted, as it is commonly used for a window. The term in England seems to carry with it the supports, imposts, jambs, and the like, on both sides of the opening. (B) One compartment or division of a building, or other structure, which consists of several similar compartments. The earliest English permanent dwellings, and barns also, although the two were often united, were built in bays, whence undoubtedly the sense C below. A house might consist of one bay, or many, and could be rented, sold, or left by will in separate bays; thus, three children might inherit each one bay of a house, and in this way the houses of early times in England, having a nearly uniform section at all points, much resembled the long house of the Iroquois Indians. The general length of the bay was about 16 feet; and it has been alleged that the measure of length, known as the rod, pole, or perch, is derived from this length of the bay. Hence, in later and more elaborate structures, the term applies to a similar division, as of a roof or floor, which is included between any two main transverse supports of a series. In such connections, the term is commonly used in combination as in bay of joists, bay of rafters. In modern times the nave or an aisle of a church, or any building divided by arcades or colonnades, is considered as divided into bays, each bay consisting of two columns, pilasters, or the like, with the space between, so that one bay of a three-aisled church consists of a piece taken across the whole building from outer wall to outer wall, including both aisles and the nave. In like manner, one compartment of any single wall or arcade of such a building is spoken of as a bay, and the decoration of a piece of wall around, and enclosing one of the windows, is sometimes spoken of as a unit. By extension, the term is sometimes applied to divisions, or compartments, of small and relatively unimportant structures, as to the divisions of a bookcase; the spaces formed by the mullions of a window; and, in engineering, to the portion, as of a chord, included between two apices of a truss. (C) By extension, a compartment or recess, as in a barn, for a special purpose, as expressed in the compound terms, "hay bay" "horse bay." (D) In plastering, that piece of the work which is included between two screeds, and which is done at one operation.

Bead, Angle: A bead in either of the above senses, applied as a finish to an angle or corner. Specifically, a strip used in place of an angle staff as a protection to the salient angle of a plastered wall, to which it is secured under the plaster, the only visible portion being a projecting molding forming a bead at the corner. By extension, a metal contrivance for the same purpose,

but having no bead and arranged so as to be quite concealed by the plaster.

Bead, Center: A flush bead molded at about the center of a board, or the like.

Bead, Cock: A bead molded or applied so as to project beyond a surface or surfaces. It is return-cocked if it occurs on the angle or arris, and quirked if flanked by a groove on each side.

Bead, Corner: Same as Angle Bead, especially in the specific sense as used in plastering.

Bead, Double: Two beads side by side, there being no other surface or molding between them.

Bead, Flush: One worked in material so that its rounded outside is flush with the general surface.

Bead, Nosing: A molding, generally semicylindrical, on the edge of a board or the like, and occupying its entire thickness. Generally placed so as to project beyond an adjoining face, as at the juncture of a tread and riser of a staircase, where the molded projection of the tread beyond the riser is the nosing.

Bead, Parting: Same as Parting Strip, especially when small, and having in part the form of a bead in sense A.

Bead, Ploughed: Same as Flush Bead.

Bead, Quirked: A bead separated from an adjoining surface by a quirk or narrow groove along one or both sides, as is common in the case of a flush bead or the like.

Bead, Rail: A cock bead when on a uniform, continuous surface, and not at an angle, reveal, or the like.

Bead, Rebate: A bead in the reentrant angle of a rebate.

Bead, Return: A bead at the edge of a return, as along the edge of the salient corner of a wall.

Bead, Staff: An angle staff of which the greater part forms a bead at the corner.

Bead Molding: Cylindrical molding with ornament resembling a string of beads. Common in Romanesque architecture.

Bead: (A) A convex rounded molding, commonly of semicircular section. Hence, by extension,--(B) A slender piece or member of wood or metal, having generally, wholly, or in part the section of a bead in sense A.

Beam, Arched: Any beam or similar member formed with an upward curve, whether of one piece bent or cut to the required curve, or whether made up of several parts secured together. A common form is the Laminated Arch which, however, acts by direct downward pressure upon its points of support and with little or no outward thrust.

Beam, Bending: A beam that bends upward or downward when an extra load is applied to it.

Beam, Binding: In floor framing, the beam which supports the bridging beams (or floor beams) above and the ceiling beams below.

Beam, Bowstring: In British usage, a simple form of the bowstring truss.

Beam, Box: An iron or steel beam, in shape like a long box with open ends, formed by two webs connected by top and bottom plates, or latticing. The webs may be either I Beams, Channel Beams, or Built Beams of plates and angles. Larger or more important ones are known as Box Girders.

Beam, Bridging: A floor beam carried by girders or binding beams as distinguished from one which spans the whole space between bearing walls.

Beam, Built: Any beam made up or built of several parts, as a Plate Beam, a Box Beam.

Beam, Bulb: An iron beam having a flange at one edge of the web and a nearly cylindrical rib or bar along the other edge; the name being given from the appearance of a section of the beam showing a cross piece at one end and a rounded expansion at the other.

Beam, Camber: A beam to which has been given a slight camber or upward crowning in the center for the purpose of counteracting any possible sagging in the future. The name is also applied in England to a beam whose upper surface is cut to a slight slope from the middle toward each end, as for nearly flat roofs.

Beam, Ceiling: A light joint or beam set to receive the lathing for a plastered ceiling. In English practice the ceiling joists are mortised into the binding beams, or notched into their under edges and spiked. In American practice ceiling joists are seldom used except for false ceiling under fireproof floors, the ceiling laths being usually nailed either directly to the under edges of the floor joists, or to furring strips crossing the joists to whose under edges they are nailed. Their use has the advantage that heavy pressure or sudden blows upon the floor above will be less apt to injure the ceiling. Such ceilings are less apt to transmit sound.

Beam, Cellular: The cellular beam or tubular bridge at one time in vogue for large bridges. It was a box beam large enough for trains to pass inside of the tube. The top, the compression member, and in a less degree the bottom, were made of cells formed by thin longitudinal partitions between their upper and lower plates. By this form of construction great stiffness and resistance to compression were obtained with a small quantity of metal. These bridges were, however, expensive to construct, difficult to repair, and remained in vogue only a short time.

Beam, Channel: A beam of iron or steel of such section that it resembles a gutter or channel. It consists of a vertical web with a flange at top and bottom on one side only. Those of the smaller dimensions are commonly known as channel bars or channel irons.

Beam, Collar: A tie beam in a roof truss, connecting two opposite principal rafters at a level above the wall plate or foot of the truss; as, for example, in buildings whose upper story extends into the roof, the ceiling being carried by the collar beam. The collar beam is thus usually a tie taking the place of the more common tie beam. It might, however, become a strut if the horizontal thrusts of the rafters were otherwise overcome as in some forms of truss.

Beam, Common: A beam to which the flooring is nailed, as distinguished from a binding joist or ceiling joist. Common joists in American practice are 2 to 3 inches thick and 8 to 12 inches deep, according to the length or span. They are ordinarily set 16 inches on centers, or 12 inches for heavy or very strong floors

Beam, Compound: Same as Built Beam.

Beam, Deck: Any beam to support a deck; specifically, same as Bulb Beam.

Beam, Hammer: In some kinds of framing, especially for steep roofs, a short beam securing the foot of the principal rafter to the brace, strut, or tie, and in a sense replacing the tie beam. The hammer beam is usually horizontal and forms part of at least two of the triangles of construction, namely, one above connected with the principal rafter, and the other below and connected with a wall piece. The object sought in replacing the tie beam by hammer beams is usually interior decorative effect.

Beam, Heading: Same as header.

Beam, I: A beam whose section approaches the form of the capital letter I in the Roman alphabet, having a web which connects the upper and lower flanges at their center lines. Those of the smaller dimensions are commonly called I Bars.

Beam, Joggle: (see Joggle)

Beam, Laced: More often Lattice Beam.

Beam, Lattice: A beam having its top and bottom flanges connected by diagonal members forming a lattice in place of a solid web; forming, in fact, a simple truss. The term is extended to include such members when constructed with what is more specifically known as Lacing.

Beam, Plate: A beam or girder built with plates of rolled iron. It is used instead of standard rolled iron or steel I Beams in cases where the local or structural conditions are such as to make the latter unavailable or insufficient for the service. Such beams are built with vertical plates called webs with angle bars riveted to them on both sides at top and bottom, forming flanges, and are further strengthened where necessary by one or more horizontal plates of the total width of the flanges at top and bottom. When, for greater strength, or to provide a width of top flange sufficient to permit a given wall or other superincumbent weight to be conveniently built or imposed thereon, two or three of such plate beams are used together, they are said to form a box beam or girder. Such girders are seldom made of greater span than 60 feet or of greater height than 5.

Beam, Straining: In a truss, a horizontal strut above the tie beam or above a line joining the feet of the rafters; especially, in a queen-post truss, the strut between the upper ends of the two queen-posts.

Beam, Strut: In a trussed structure, a horizontal member acting as a strut; a straining beam or a collar beam.

Beam, T: A beam whose section approaches the form of the capital letter T in the Roman alphabet.

Beam, Tie: See Tie.

Beam, Top: Same as Collar Beam.

Beam, Z: A beam whose section is nearly that of the letter Z of the Roman alphabet, having a web perpendicular to two flanges which it connects by their opposite edges. Those of the smaller dimension are commonly called Z bars.

Beam, Truss: Any beam built up of members, as a truss. The term is, however, usually restricted to mean a simple beam which is strengthened by the addition of two or more subordinate members as by means of a bent tension rod secured to the two ends of the beam and connecting one or more vertical struts beneath its under side.

Beam Hanger: A contrivance serving the purpose of a stirrup, but more elaborate and of better finish.

Beam Spread: The angle enclosed by two lines which intersect the candlepower distribution curve at the points where the candlepower is equal to ten percent of its maximum.

Beam: (A) A transverse horizontal timber used in roof construction. Horizontal timbers supporting floor or ceiling joists. A piece or member of which the transverse dimensions are small relative to its length; intended generally to be supported at two or more points to resist forces acting in a direction normal to its axis; but sometimes secured at one end only and sometimes acting as a member of a truss, in which case its purpose may be that of a strut; but always occupying a more or less horizontal position. By extension, however, the term is still used to designate any piece of a form intended primarily for the purpose described although put to another use: thus, a steel column may be constructed of channel beams, which would then be set on end. Beams of wood or stone are usually

rectangular in cross section, or nearly so. Those of iron or steel have different cross sections, but are generally composed of a top and a bottom flange connected by a thin vertical web. The most common forms are the I Beam, the Channel Beam, the Z Beam, and the Deck or Bulb Beam. Iron and steel beams are now rolled in one piece up to a depth of 2 feet. The larger sizes are made up of several pieces, and known as built beams and box beams. A large beam is frequently known as a Girder, irrespective of its use. (B) Large, horizontal cylinders or spools. Warp yarns are wound on beams and located on line in back of the weaving operation.

Bearer: Any small subordinate horizontal member, generally one of a series, to support another member or structure, as one of several small beams to carry a gutter.

Bearing Plates: In pin-connected framing, reinforcing plates riveted to the web of a beam or a chord at a joint, to thicken the web and give greater bearing surface to the pin which connects the post or brace to the beam or chord.

Bearing: (A) That part of a lintel, beam, or similar horizontal weight-carrying member which rests upon a column, pier, or wall. Thus, it may be required that a beam of a certain size, and with a certain span, should have at each end an 8-inch bearing. (B) The whole length or span of a lintel, girder, or similar structure between the two points of support, that is the whole distance between the two bearings, in sense A. Of these two meanings, the second is the one most often seen in non-technical writing, but in specifications and the like the word is more commonly limited to the signification A, and the word span is used for the distance between the two points. (C) Supporting, sustaining. Said chiefly of a wall or partition as distinguished from those which merely enclose and do not support floors or the like.

Bed: (A) To give a bed to, as a stone. (B) To lay or set on a bed, as when a stone is said to be "well bedded," i.e., fixed solidly upon the substructure. (C) The prepared soil or layer of cement or mortar on, or in, which a piece of material is laid, especially in masonry. (D) That face, more or less horizontal, of a stone, brick, or the like, which is in contact with a bed in the sense A, or prepared for that purpose, whether

beneath or on top. Such faces are known respectively as the upper and lower bed. By extension, and where no mortar is used, the upper or under flat surface of a stone prepared for building. Also the under surface of a shingle, tile, or similar piece of roofing material.

Belfry: The upper room of a tower where bells are hung. Also called a bell tower. Timber frame on which bells are hung in a belfry.

Bell Gable: A frame fastened to a roof to hold bells.

Bell-pull: A piece of rope or cloth that pulls a bell and causes it to ring.

Bema: A speakers or readers platform. Used in classical, church, and synagogue architecture.

Bench Mark: A fixed reference mark from which heights and levels are reckoned in surveying or in laying out grounds and buildings. It is usually indicated by a notch or mark on a stone or stake firmly set at a given point of the plan.

Berm: A level area separating a ditch from a bank.

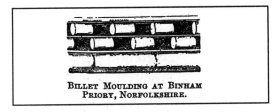

BILLET MOULDING AT BINHAM PRIORY, NORFOLKSHIRE.

Billet: Molding made up of several bands of raised cylinders or square pieces at regular intervals. Common in Romanesque architecture.

Black and White Work: Building with a frame of timber and with filling between the frames of rough masonry of any kind or even with double plastering on oak laths. The common appearance of houses built in this way throughout England during five or six centuries was nearly always that of black or gray bands alternating with white spaces, the total amount of walling being nearly equally divided between the two tints.

Blind Tracery: Tracery applied to wall surfaces and wood panels. Common in Gothic architecture.

Blister: A defect in the form of a slight projection of a surface detached from the body of the material, caused in manufacturing or by weather or other agencies, as the protuberance sometimes formed on the face of a casting, due to the presence of an air bubble just below the surface; or the loose, slightly raised portions of a coat of paint which have become detached from the material to which the paint has been applied, due to defective workmanship or other causes.

Block, Hollow: A terra cotta slab or large brick made with an opening or several openings in its body; usually for purposes of ventilation, or for lightness or economy where great strength is not needed: in those used for ventilation there are two general sorts--those which when put together form a continuous tube for the passage of a current of air, and those which are intended merely to provide an air space to prevent the passage of moisture from the outside to the inside of a wall, or as a means of insulation in fireproofing. The term "block" is commonly used instead of brick to describe such building material made of baked clay, and considerable larger than the usual bricks.

Block, Concrete: Concrete blocks used in the construction of buildings that are hollow or solid.

Block: (A) A piece of stone or terra cotta prepared, or partly prepared, for building. (B) A mass projecting from a larger piece of stone, as in some unfinished masonry of the Greeks. (C) In carpentry or joiner's work any small, more or less symmetrical, piece of wood, used for whatever purpose, as behind a wainscot, or other work which is to stand out from a wall; under any horizontal member to give it a proper level; in the angle between the sides of a box; the top and front rail of a chest of drawers or cabinet, or the like; a traditional means of giving stiffness or support where there is no room for braced framing. (D) A row or mass of buildings closely connected together, or a single structure which perhaps divided by party walls contains a number of stores or shops with dwellings above them, or dwellings only, or small apartment houses. (In this sense, peculiarly American.) (E) In a city or the like, where streets are near together, the whole space within and enclosed by three or four streets so as to present a front of houses upon each of those streets. Hence, by extension, the length of such a block upon any one street; thus, we say that in the upper part of New York City twenty blocks, taken with the streets between them, make up a mile. The city block is capable of refined treatment, first in a strictly

architectural sense, as when the exterior fronts are treated either according to a common design, elaborated in advance, or when succeeding builders of separate narrow fronts are careful to conform one to the other, not necessarily by strict imitation of style, height, or the like, but by intelligent adaptation of the newer to the older fronts. This is very rare, except when, as in Paris, under the authority of the municipality, the heights are kept severely limited, and the regulations as to windows and the like are enforced; or when, as in Nuremberg, an authoritative commission regulates the style to be observed in all designs. On the other hand, the interior of a block is capable of a great deal of skilful treatment, rather in the way of landscape architecture than of architecture in the usual sense. Thus, in certain blocks of London, and a few in the United States, the whole space enclosed by the rear walls of the houses is opened into a kind of garden with trees planted with some reference to general effect, and the divisions between the back yards are to a certain extent effaced, at least to all appearance. Lots are often sold with strict limits as to the front line of the house, so as to leave a small courtyard or open area for the whole length of the block; but the same regulation must be extended to the interior if it is desired to prevent libraries, dining rooms, and the like, from being built to the very extreme end of each separate lot, thereby destroying the interior garden. (F) To set or provide with a block or blocks in sense of Block, C; to secure or place in position by means of such blocks; to perform the operation of blocking. Commonly used with the adverb, as block up, block out.

Blocking Course: A projecting stone cornice at the base of a building. In classical architecture, a plain stone course with a cornice at the top of a building.

Blow Molding: Thermoplastic materials formed by stretching and hardening plastic to a mold. Molten thermoplastic is shaped and put into a mold, air blown, cooled, and removed from the mold.

Blueprinting: A process of inexpensively reproducing an original drawing. This process allows the designer, who draws plans, details and other types of drawings on transparent or translucent paper, to have one or 100 copies to give to the client and

contractors, and still protect the valuable original.

Board Measure: The standard system for the measurement of lumber. A board foot is a square foot one inch thick, and hence the equivalent of 144 cubic inches. A 3" x 4" stud measures one board foot per foot of length; a 6" x 12" beam measures 6 board feet per foot of length. No allowance is made for loss by sawing, planing, or other dressing; 7/8' planed boards are reckoned as 1 inch thick. Lumber is sold by the "M" or thousand board feet. The board foot, the "hundred," and the "M" or thousand are the only units in common use.

Board: (A) A piece of lumber before gluing for width or thickness. (B) A slab of wood cut to a more or less uniform shape, and thin as compared to its width and length. Specifically, such a piece of lumber not more than about 1 1/4' inches thick. (C) To cover or sheath with boards. In housebuilding in the United States, a frame structure is said to be boarded when the frame has been covered in with the sheathing boards, previous to the addition of clapboards or shingles.

Boarding: (A) Boards in general, or a quantity of boards taken together. (B) The act of covering a surface with boards, usually by nailing to a frame of wood. (C) The covering or thickness of boards applied, as in B. Thus, the boarding of the exterior of a frame house in the United States is commonly double, first the sheathing and then the siding.

Boast: To shape stone roughly in preparation for subsequent finer dressing.

Boasted Work: Rough blocked stonework prior to carving. Masonry finished with a boaster chisel.

Body: (A) The larger, or more central mass of a building having varied parts, as a church. (B) The shaft, or plain upright part, of a pillar or pier of any sort. (C) Solidity, mass, thickness, and the like, taken in the abstract; thus, it may be said that such a paint lacks body. (D) The solid, firm, or full feel of a fabric.

Bolt: A pin or rod used either to secure two or more parts or members permanently together; or movable, as for a temporary fastening; or fixed, to afford a more or less temporary support or means of attachment. More specifically; (A) A pin or bar, generally of wrought iron or steel, to secure parts or members together, having a head worked on one end and a screw thread and nut at the other, or sometimes nuts at both ends. Distinguished from a rod as connecting two or more members in immediate contact, and, also, as being shorter. (B) A pin, hook, or large screw driven or let into a wall, or the like, as a means--generally temporary--of support or suspension. Hardly to be distinguished from a spike or screw in the ordinary sense, except as being larger or of more elaborate form.

Boltel: (A) In medieval architecture, a convex rounded molding. (B) By extension from the above meaning, the coping of a convex rounded portion of the wall of a gable, generally forming a quadrant.

Bond: The connection of two or more parts or members which overlap and are made to adhere more or less closely; thence, a piece or pieces used for that purpose. Specifically; (A) In carpentry, (1) the securing or framing of two or more timbers together by means of a third crossing them; (2) the timbers, considered collectively, placed in or on the walls, and which act to stiffen and bind the parts of a building, as wall plates, templates.

(B) In masonry, (1) the tie or binding of the various parts or pieces made by laying one piece across two or more pieces or parts; (2) a piece of material used for that purpose; hence, (3) the entire system of bonding or breaking joints as used in a masonry structure, for example, a wall may be said to be built in English bond. Incorrectly, the securing or holding together the parts of a masonry structure by the mortar or similar adhesive material.

(C) In roofing, (1) the amount by which one slate, tile, or shingle overlaps the second course below. (2) Sometimes the distance from the nail of one to the lower edge of the course above. In bonding masonry, the following names are given to the various pieces of stone or brick:-- Binder; Header, one laid lengthwise across a wall, generally perpendicular with the face. Perpend, in stonework, a binder extending entirely through, from face to face (French *parpaing*). Stretcher, one laid lengthwise parallel with the face. Through, same as perpend. The various systems of bonding are as given in the subtitles, in the definitions of which cross references have not been thought essential.

Boring: In preparations for building, a process of examining the soils or rocks beneath the surface where a building is to be erected. Boring is properly limited to the softer materials alone, such as sand, gravel, clay, and the like; but when a rock is struck it is drilled, and this is included in the general term.

For the purpose of boring, different augers are used, even a common pump auger turned by a long bar screwed to its head and slowly moved by several men; but for a proper examination of the materials beneath the surface it is customary to use an auger working through a pipe which retains a core of the excavated materials in their original relative positions. If careful note is taken of the exact depth to which the pipes had been sunk when each separate sample of the soil was collected, a fair notion of the soils beneath can be obtained. When a larger and a smaller pipe may be used together, the smaller one is put within the larger, and water is forced into the space between the two pipes; the materials below, if divisible and not too firmly indurated, are then washed up through the inner pipe and may be collected at the surface.

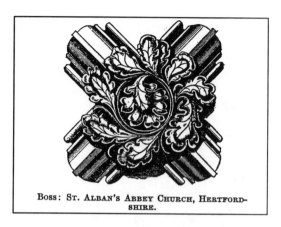

BOSS: ST. ALBAN'S ABBEY CHURCH, HERTFORD-SHIRE.

Boss: (A) A projecting mass of stone, usually not large and commonly intended to be cut away after the completion of the work. (B) A mass projecting, as in A, but intended as a permanent feature; thus, in Gothic architecture, the molded sill course of a window, or a row of windows, is often terminated by sculptured projections of the sort. The most common use of the term is for the carved keystones of Gothic vaults. Where the different ribs meet at the top of the vault such a piece of stone (called by the French *clef*) is an almost essential feature, and this, if treated in a decorative way, is the boss. Those of the thirteenth century are sometimes of great richness. In later times they often took the form of the pendant.

Bottom: The soil or other natural resisting material on which a

building is founded, as at the bottom of an excavation or on which piles may bear.

Boulevard: A wide street with plants or trees down the middle.

Box-frame: Concrete construction in which the load is carried by cross walls.

Brace, Angle: A brace set across the corner of a more or less rectangular structure, as at the corner of a frame house.

Brace, Batter: The inclined braces at the end of a truss, as of a Pratt truss.

Brace, Counter: In a truss an extra or supplementary brace crossing the main brace. It is introduced in those panels which are exposed to change of shape in two directions.

Brace, Portal: In ironwork, a brace approaching the form of a knee inserted in the angle between a vertical and a horizontal member to resist lateral pressure. Being commonly bent approximately to a quarter-circle, a pair of them, placed so as to face each other, will produce the effect of an arched portal.

Brace, Principal; Principal Sway Brace: A brace to stiffen a principal rafter or its supporting structure; as, especially, in the angle between a tiebeam and its end-support.

Brace, Purlin: In carpentry, a brace from a roof truss to relieve or stiffen a purlin between its bearings upon the principals.

Brace, Sway: A brace inserted to prevent sideways motion, as under the influence of wind; therefor, usually horizontal in position or in the plane of the main structure. This term, common in bridge building, is rare in architecture.

Brace, Wind: A sway brace designed primarily to resist the lateral action of wind.

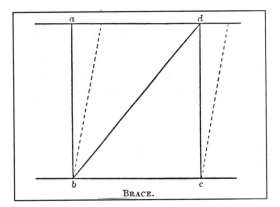

BRACE.

Brace: A piece or member, generally long as compared to its lateral dimensions, used to stiffen or steady another member or structure;

specifically:--A bar introduced into a framework to prevent distortion or change of shape, usually a diagonal in a quadrilateral. It may act either by tension or by compression. The quadrilateral abcd may change its shape by the rotation of its sides about the joints. If the rigid diagonal brace *bd* is introduced and firmly attached, deformation is rendered impossible except by rupture of the parts. If the rectangle is exposed to deforming forces in two directions, i.e., to the right or to the left in the diagram; a single rigid brace firmly attached to the frame will prevent change of shape, but it is customary in such case to introduce two diagonals, both ties or both struts or compression members, as the case may be; which facilitates construction. If the four sides of the quadrilateral are rigid members, the diagonals will be ties. If two of the opposite sides are tension members, the braces will be struts.

Braces: Subsidiary roof timbers set diagonally to strengthen the frames.

Bracing: The operation of strengthening a framed or other structure by means of braces; or any system or aggregation of braces. The general principle upon which bracing depends for its efficiency is

that of the triangle, whose shape cannot be changed without breaking, bending, or altering the length of one or more of its sides.

Bracket: A member prepared for carrying a weight which overhangs or projects, as a projecting story of a building, or a shelf. This is the general term; and although it would not be applied, often, to a cantilever, a corbel, a cul-de-lampe, or a modillion except carelessly, it covers all varieties which have no specific names of their own. The action of the bracket is twofold: it pulls outward along the line of the horizontal top bar or edge, and presses inward more solidly at the foot. If, therefore, a bracket is secured to a wall along the whole height of its vertical member, the more the horizontal member above is loaded, as with a balcony, bay window, or the like, the more of a pull is exercised upon the wall immediately below this projecting member. This may even become dangerous; and it is, therefore, customary to make the bracket a part of a floor or other horizontal member which can resist a strong outward tendency. The term is applied also to small movable objects which project from walls so as to resemble distantly the architectural bracket. Thus, a gas fixture for a wall opening, and, equally, a support for a bust, or vase, hung upon a hook, received the name.

Brake: A machine that allows wide sheets or plates to be bent.

Break: A change in the continuity of a surface or member. Thus, a projecting chimney breast forms, on either side, a break in the wall.

Breakfront: A cabinet with drawers on the bottom and glass doors on the top. The middle portion is a few inches extended from the sides.

Breast: (A) The projecting portion of a chimney, especially when projecting into a room or other apartment. (B) The under side of a hand rail, beam, rafter, or the like.

(C) That portion of a wall which is between a window sill and the floor.

Bressumer: Horizontal timber carrying a wall.

Brewster Chair: A seventeenth century armchair with a rush or plank seat, posts, and spindles. The chair is American Jacobean style and was named for William Brewster who was a Plymouth colonist.

Brick, Face: A brick that is used on the exposed surface because of a special quality in texture or color.

Brick: (A) A regularly shaped piece of clay hardened in the sun or by the heat of a kiln and intended for building; commonly one of very many pieces of uniform size. The term is usually limited to pieces of clay not very thin and flat, which latter are called tiles; the ordinary brick are, as in parts of the United States, about 2 1/2' x 4" x 8", or, as in parts of Europe, about 2 5/8''x 4 3/8' x 9". Bricks made for facework, as it is called, that is to say, the smoother and more elegant facing of the exterior of a wall, are made of many shapes and colors and commonly laid with mortar joints much smaller than those between the common bricks in the same wall. Molded bricks are made in a great number of patterns, and so arranged as to form, when laid up in the wall, continuous lines of molding, curves of an arch, and the like, or patterns in relief, and even to the extent of having a raised leafage or the like upon their faces. (B) The material, baked clay, in small pieces in a general sense.

Bricklaying: The art and practice of laying bricks in masonry. As the purpose of bricklaying, when simple and confined to ordinary walls, is merely to produce a solid, almost homogeneous mass of small pieces of baked clay held together by strong mortar, the chief training given to a bricklayer is to lay bricks rapidly with fair accuracy and tolerable neatness.

Face bricks are laid by men especially trained for that purpose, or who have become especially skillful. The more difficult parts of bricklaying are the laying up of flues, where no lining, as of earthenware pipe, is to be used; the building of the throats of chimneys, upon the accurate adjustment of which much depends; and the doing of corbelled-out work with chimney tops and the like, all of which may be considered, together with the

laying of molded brick, as unusual and ornamental parts of the trade.

BRIDGE (ROMAN) AT ALCÁNTARA, SPAIN.

Bridge: A structure spanning a river, ravine, etc. with space below to allow passage underneath.

Bridging: (A) A piece, or pieces, of scantling, or heavier timber, placed transversely between other timbers to stiffen them and to distribute the weight of a load more evenly on them. (B) The setting of bridging pieces, or of any pieces which are to serve as struts or stiffeners between parallel beams. When the bridging between the floor joists forms a series of $x's$, it is often called Cross Bracing and Cross Bridging, in the United States.

Bristol Board, High Surface (Smooth or Plate Finish): A uniformly smooth finish overall; takes the most delicate line techniques in pen or pencil.

Bristol Board, Medium Surface (Kid or Vellum Finish): A "toothy," slightly textured finish for almost any technique; line and wash, air brush, tempera, acrylic, pastel, etc. Either surface withstands repeated erasures and reworking.

Brownstone: Dark brown or reddish brown sandstone used for construction in eastern North America. The name of nineteenth century eastern U.S. houses built from brownstone.

Buckle: To bulge or curve under excessive strain; to deviate from the normal. Used to describe walls and other members which suffer deflection as under extreme load; of metal plates; of boards, and the like, which warp or twist because too thin or light.

Buckled Plate: A metal plate, generally square, stamped or wrought with a slight domical convexity, leaving a flat rim with straight edges. Laid on iron beams, they are commonly used on account of their stiffness, as a foundation for fireproof floors.

Buckled: In a special sense, corrugated; said of thin metal plates. The term was originally applied to corrugations of a peculiar form, connected with a patent.

Building Paper: Paper used in immediate connection with building, usually either to provide warmth, or to serve as a deafening. Many patent papers are in the market, the general tendency of such manufacture being toward heavy and soft material, as thickness is needed while strength would be unimportant. The use in the United States of paper applied between the first sheathing and the outer clapboards in all kinds of frame buildings has proved most useful to the comfort of the houses so protected.

Building System: Means plans, specifications, and documentation for a system of manufactured buildings or for a type or a system of building components, which may include structural, electrical, mechanical, plumbing, and fire protection systems and other building systems affecting life safety.

Bungalow: A small house with a verandah.

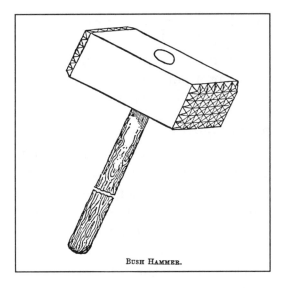

BUSH HAMMER.

Bush Hammer: In stone dressing, a hammer used in finishing the harder stones. It has a prismatic head, the ends of which are square, and divided into a number of pyramidal points.

Bush-hammering: A process of rough texturing concrete after it is set. A bush-hammer with a grooved head is used to texture the surface.

Buttress, Angle: Two buttresses that meet at 90 degree angles of a building.

Buttress, Clasping: A buttress which encases an angle.

Buttress, Diagonal: A buttress at a right angle formed by two walls.

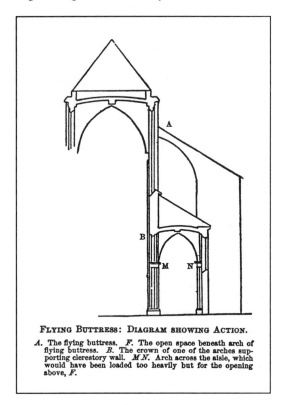

FLYING BUTTRESS: DIAGRAM SHOWING ACTION.

A. The flying buttress. F. The open space beneath arch of flying buttress. B. The crown of one of the arches supporting clerestory wall. M N. Arch across the aisle, which would have been loaded too heavily but for the opening above, F.

Buttress, Flying: A half-arch or arch which transmits the thrust of a vault or roof to an outer buttress.

Buttress, Lateral: A buttress standing on axis with one wall at the corner of a building.

Buttress, Setback: A buttress setback from the angle.

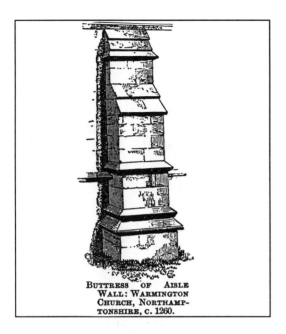

BUTTRESS OF AISLE
WALL: WARMINGTON
CHURCH, NORTHAMP-
TONSHIRE, c. 1260.

Buttress: Brickwork or masonry
projecting from a wall for structural
lateral reinforcement. Used in
Gothic architecture to distribute
lateral loads from arches, vaults and
roofs.

C

Cabriole Leg: A style of furniture that curves outward toward the top and inward toward the bottom, usually resembling an animal's paw.

Caisson: (A) As used for building upon pile foundations or other firm bottom under water, a water-tight box in which the masonry is built, and is then lowered into its place. The floor is made strong enough to carry the weight of the masonry, the sides are detachable, and are taken off when the caisson rests upon the bottom. The caisson is sometimes made large enough to be buoyant with its load of masonry and is sunk by letting in water, is sometimes lowered by chains from a fixed platform, but usually it is floated into position and sinks as the masonry is built in it.

(B) Generally with the qualifying term pneumatic or compressed air--a device for sinking foundations under water or in soil containing much water, or too soft to be supported by other means. It is in form an air-tight box the size of the pier to be built upon it; the bottom is open, the top is strongly floored to carry the weight of the masonry. It is sometimes framed of wood, but for architectural building it is generally made of steel plates and beams. Entrance and exit are by means of an air lock; materials are generally supplied through a separate air lock. In use, the caisson is loaded sufficiently to overcome the friction of the earth on its sides, and the lifting power of the compressed air within it. This loading is usually the masonry which it is to support. The air is introduced under a pressure sufficient to exclude or expel the water or fluid earth entering under the lower edge. The earth in the center and under the edges is excavated by men working in the compressed air, and is lifted out in buckets through an air lock, or blown out through special pipes by compressed air or by a water jet. As weight is added above, and the supporting earth beneath is removed by excavation aided at times by reducing the air pressure, the caisson gradually stinks until the lower or cutting edge rests upon the rock or other surface upon which it is to remain. It is then filled solid with concrete, and the air locks are removed for use elsewhere. The masonry upon it has meantime been carried above water, so as to be accessible when the caisson has come to rest. The air pressure is generally taken at half a pound to the square inch for every foot in depth of water, although this is in excess of their actual relation. (C) A sunken panel in a ceiling.

Camarin: A small chapel behind the altar of Spanish churches.

Camber Piece; Slip: A piece of wood having its upper surface slightly curved upward; used as a centering in building flat arches so as to give the intrados a slight camber; sometimes a mere board with one edge cut to a convex are of a very long radius, or a barrel stave.

Camber: A slight rise or upward curve of an otherwise horizontal, or apparently horizontal, piece or structure. In a steel truss having apparently parallel, horizontal chords, the pieces composing the upper chord are usually made slightly longer between joints than the corresponding parts below; the result being a slight invisible camber, by which the tendency to sag is overcome. A so-called flat arch is usually built with an intrados having a camber.

Came: A metal strip used in leaded window lights.

Campanile: In Italian, a bell tower; hence, a bell tower of Italian design or general character, especially a church tower more or less completely separated from the rest of the building, and generally having no buttress nor any marked break in its outline, which is square, unbuttressed, plain, and with nearly all its decorative effect near the top in connection with the belfry chamber. Such towers are abundant in Italy during all the medieval epoch, and their general character was preserved in the Renaissance and post-Renaissance styles. Among the largest existing are those of the cathedral of Cremona in Lombardy, of S. Mark's church in Venice, and of the Piazza dei Signori in Verona. The exquisitely graceful campanile of S. Zeno of Verona has a two-story belfry, and it has been noted by recent observers that its sides are not strictly vertical, but have a slight entasis.

Cancello: A lattices screen used in early churches to separate the choir from the main area of the church.

Candelabrum: (A) In Latin, a lampstand. Some of those known to us are very small and low; but those which are of interest architecturally are high and of considerable pretensions. Some of these are of bronze, and very slender; but others are cut in marble or finegrained stone, and are sometimes 5 or 6 feet high, and very massive. The forms of these last have entered somewhat into neoclassic decoration. (B) A candlestick made decorative by wrought work, in metal, enamel, or the like; especially one having several sockets for candles, and of large size. (C) A modified column, small and decorated, and usually engaged. The typical form is that of a rapidly tapering shaft with a florid capital, the whole emerging from a cluster of leafage below. (D) By still further extension, an upright piece of scroll work in painted decoration, mosaic, or the like. To receive this title, which is vague in its application, the scroll pattern should have a formal central rib nearly straight and nearly vertical, from which the scrolls are thrown off on either side.

Canopy: (A) A rooflike structure usually supported on pillars or projecting from a wall, and serving rather a decorative than a protective purpose. It may be movable, as

when carried above an important person in a procession, and may consist of an awning of silk or other material supported on poles; or it may be of light material and permanently placed, as above a bedside, whether supported by the posts or hung from the ceiling; or it may be of solid material. In a Gothic niche, the canopy is the most important part. (B) Bed drapery that hangs from posts or the ceiling.

Cant: (A) The angle of inclination of a piece or member to the general surface, especially to the horizontal, hence,--(B) A portion or surface which makes an oblique angle with adjoining parts, especially a slope of considerable relative extent.

Cantilever: A member intended to support an overhanging weight, like a bracket; but generally of large size and having a projection much greater than its height; especially, a projecting beam--one which is fixed in a wall or other support at one end, the other end being unsupported. Applied to a bridge or a beam, it means an end projecting beyond the support.

Cap: (A)The crowning or terminal feature of a vertical member of any structure, either fitting closely upon it or extending somewhat beyond it in horizontal dimensions; thus distinguished from a Finial. The capital of a column, pilaster, or pier, the surbase or cornicelike finish of a pedestal, the cast-iron head of an iron or timber post, the crowning horizontal timber of a stud partition, a timber bolster on a post to diminish the unsupported span of the superstructure, are alike called caps, and the term is also used of a wall coping, door lintel, or handrail as of a balustrade. (B) The top feature of a wind-mill or conical roof.

Caphouse: A small superstructure to a stair leading to a parapet walk.

Capital, Basket: A hemispherical capital decorated with a wicker basket-like design. Prominent in Byzantine architecture.

Capital, Bell: Capital in the form of a reversed bell. The bell is often decorated with carvings.

Capital, Block: Capital cut from a cube with the lower parts rounded off to the circular shaft. Prominent in Romanesque and Byzantine architecture.

Capital, Crocket: A capital formed with stylized leaves with ending rolled over as small volutes. Prominent in Early Gothic architecture.

Capital, Cube: See block capital.

Capital, Cushion: See block capital.

Capital, Double: (A) One furnished with a Dosseret, A. (B) One as described in the account of Persian columns in the article above.

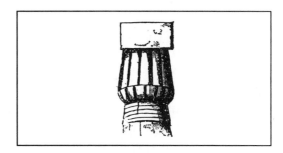

Capital, Lotus: A capital in the form of a lotus bud. An Egyptian style.

Capital, Palm: A capital in the form of the crown of a palm tree. An Egyptian style.

Capital, Protomai: A capital, usually with half-figures of animals projecting from the corners.

Capital, Scalloped: A block capital in which the single lunette on each face is formed into one or more truncated cones.

CAPITAL FROM THE TEMPLE OF KARNAK.

Capital: The head or crown of a column.

Car: The platform or enclosed chamber of an elevator or lift.

Carillon: A chime of bells. The French term signifying a number of bells grouped together, and so differing in size and tone as to be capable of producing musical combinations of sound. In English, as in French, the term is extended to mean the sound itself, especially when a large number of bells is employed. The most remarkable carillons are those in Belgium and the Netherlands. It is stated that a church in Delft had once a thousand bells, but that number is now much reduced. Several of those in Belgium have more than 150 bells, the smallest of which is scarcely larger than the dinner bell of a country tavern. Ordinarily the hammers of the bells are moved by means of wires attached to a piece of machinery with a revolving drum. The mingling of sound is not very artistically planned, and is rather a pleasant jangle of separately agreeable notes than a concerted piece of music. In some of the towns of Belgium the carillon is rung every quarter of an hour.

Carpenter: A worker in wood; especially one who does the larger and rougher work, as of building construction, and as distinguished from a joiner and cabinetmaker.

Carpentry: The work of a carpenter. Also, the result of such work; building in wood, or woodwork in general. Carpentry is sometimes distinguished from Framing as referring rather to the smaller members of a building, as window frames, stairs, if not highly finished, flooring, and the like; it is distinguished from joinery and cabinetmaking as being rougher and dealing rather with the essential parts of a structure than the more decorative parts without which the building might still exist.

Carriage: (A) An inclined beam or stringpiece for supporting a stair. (B) In a lumber mill, the movable framework which carries the log or plank and feeds it to the saw or plane.

Carving: (A) Cutting in wood, stone, or other resistant material requiring the use of a sharp tool; especially, ornamental cutting, whether in relief or in intaglio. (B) A work or piece of sculpture as described.

Caryatid: A column made in the form of a female figure. Columns or pilasters carved all or partially as human figures.

Cascade: In the architectural sense, an artificial waterfall so arranged as to form part of an architectural or decorative composition. The most important example is that in the garden of the Royal Palace, at Caserta, near Naples.

Case Door: A frame consisting of jamb pieces and lintel or head framed or nailed together, to one side of which the door is hung, and in which it closes; that face of the frame or case having a rebate so that the door when closed into the rebate shall be flush with the wall, or in a plane parallel with the face of the wall. In thin walls and partitions the case is as thick as the partition, and finished with a trim on either side of the latter. In thick walls the case finishes with a trim on one side, and a bead or molding against the masonry or plastered jam on the other.

Case: (A) A box, enclosure, or hollow receptacle, as the space in which a stairway is built: a staircase. (B) Same as Casing. (C) The carcass of structural framework of a house or other building. (Rare in United States.)

Casemate: A vaulted room built in the thickness of ramparts or fortification and used as a battery or barracks.

Casement: (A) A window having hinged or pivoted sash, opening either outward or inward. In North Germany many such windows open outward, and this is preferred, except where it is desired to put up secondary or outer fixed sash (forming "double windows") in winter. English country houses were commonly fitted with light iron sash in very small casements. These also opened outward, and were held by long hooks or some other form of sash-holder. This fashion has been revived of late. (B) One leaf or swinging frame forming part of such a window, and thus in British usage distinguished from a sash. In the United States, usually called casement sash. (C) In medieval architecture, a deep, hollow molding similar to the Scotia of classic architecture.

Casement; French: A casement having two meeting hinged leaves opening inward, secured usually when closed by an Espagnolette. This is almost the only form of window used in France, and is common throughout Europe. The difficulty of making such casements tight against driving storms is overcome in France by careful workmanship. The meeting rails form a large semicircular tongue and groove, forced tightly one into the other by closing. The sill joint is protected either by a drip molding on the bottom rails overhanging the edge of the wooden stool, or by a hinged brass drip, which, on closing the window, folds down over the stool. In the United States French casements are chiefly used to give access to balconies or verandas.

Casing: In general, the exterior covering of a structure or member of a structure; a shell or boxing of some superior material, as the mahogany casing of a ceiling beam. Specifically, in the United States the boxing or frame about an opening-- that portion which is parallel to the general surrounding surface, and therefore usually at right angles to the jambs. It may be structural, as those parts which form the inside and the outside of a cased frame, or decorative, as the trim or architrave of a door. A door or window set into a wall.

Casino: An ornamental pavilion on the grounds of a larger house. A building for gambling.

Cast in Place: Concrete casts that are made on the construction site.

Castellated: Decorated with battlements.

Castle: A fortified house or living structure.

Castrum: A Roman military camp.

Catacomb: An underground cemetery or series of linked underground passages.

Catch: A contrivance for automatically securing a door, shutter, or a similar movable leaf by the action of gravity or of a spring. In some of its more elaborate forms hardly to be distinguished from a latch or spring lock.

Cathedra: The bishop's chair in a cathedral church. Usually placed behind the high altar.

Cathedral: (more properly Cathedral Church). The church in which is set up the Bishop's Throne or Cathedra. This church may be considered as the bishop's Throne Room; or, if the Choir be considered as the throne room, then the cathedral with Chapter House and other accessories, and the actual residence of the bishop, together with the Cloisters and other enclosed spaces, may be considered as the Episcopal Palace, resembling a royal or grand ducal palace in having rooms for business and ceremony combined in the same building with the residence of the prince and his officers and attendants. The cathedral itself is not necessarily large nor splendid, nor is there any architectural style or character which can be said to belong to it in a peculiar sense. In Athens, the old cathedral remains one of the smallest churches in the world, and capable of containing a congregation of only a few score.

Caulcole: Stalk rising from the leaves of a Corinthian capital.

Caulking: (A) The act or method of securing the end of a timber, like a girder or tie beam, to another on which it rests at right angles (as the wall plate or sill) by means of a cog hold. (B) The operation or method of rendering a joint tight, as against water or gas, by driving into its interstices with a chisel or other tool some plastic or elastic substance, as oakum and tar in the decks of ships, lead in the hubs of soil pipes, etc. (C) In boiler work and hydraulic work a process for making a joint stream or water tight by upsetting the edges of the steel or iron plates. (Written also Calking, Cauking, Cocking, Cogging.)

Ceiling: (A) The covering of a wall surface, especially on the interior; or of the under side of a floor; the material used being always supposed to be a simple and ordinary one. Thus, ceiling is of thin boards or of lath and plaster, but never of tile, nor is the term applied to the surface afforded by the solid material of a wall or floor; except as under B. (B) By extension from A, the under side of a floor which provides the roofing or enclosure at top of a room or other space below. In this case, it is the surface alone which is designated without reference to material.

Ceiling: Beam: A ceiling, generally of wood, made in imitation of exposed floor beams with the flooring showing between. Hence, sometimes, the under side of a floor, showing the actual beams, and finished to form a ceiling.

Ceilings: The overhead surface of a room.

Cell: Compartment of a rib vault or groin. A sleeping room in a monastery.

Cella: Main body of a classical temple. It housed the cult image.

Cellar, Earth: A cellar in sense B above, excavated in the face of a steep slope of ground, and at its foot, so as to have a floor at about the level of the ground in front. Such a chamber will be nearly enclosed on three sides by the natural soil, and roof being usually boarded, but perhaps of earth supported from below. A common means in the United States of obtaining a cool storage place.

Cellar, Sub: In a building having more than one cellar as described under definition A above, the lower or one of the lower underground stories. The great height of the recent sky scrapers of the United States has made it desirable in many cases to extend the foundations to solid rock, as in New York City. The foundations will then reach a depth of perhaps 30 or 40 feet, allowing the construction of three or more stories below the street level. The uppermost story will then usually be known as the cellar, and lower ones as subcellars.

Cellar, Wine: A room arranged for the reception of wine and other fermented or distilled liquors. The primary requisite is that it should have a very even temperature, the warmth of the atmosphere within it changing gradually, if at all. Ventilation is only needed so far as dampness is to be avoided, and a very slow changing of the air should be sufficient for this. Excellent results have followed, when the general cellar space is dry, but shutting off a piece of it completely without any provision whatever for the changing of air. It is customary to provide a separate room for wine, etc., in casks and for that which is bottled. The room for casks should be spacious enough to allow of the fining, bottling, etc. of the liquor contained in the casks. The cellar for bottled liquors should be fitted up with shelves, although recent devices of light ironwork, wire, etc., and also of baked clay in the form of hollow tiles, have been made for the same purpose. With ordinary wooden shelving, a distinction must be made between bottles that are to set up and those which are to be laid on their sides; for these latter it is good to arrange the shelving so as to make diagonal compartments like very large pigeonholes set cornerwise, with one of the angles pointing downward.

Cellar: (A) The space below the ground story or the basement story of a building, enclosed by the foundation walls, and therefore wholly, or almost entirely, below the surface of the surrounding ground. The distinction between cellar and basement story is not absolute, and, in some cases, may depend on the use to which such a space is put, as much as on its relative situation. Thus, in an English-basement house, the front portion of the lowest, nearly subterranean, story will frequently be without windows, and used merely for storage of fuel and the like, and will therefore be referred to as a cellar; but the same story might be equally well provided with large windows opening into an area, and would then be used as a living room or for domestic offices, and would be called a basement story. Hence, as such a space is commonly used for storage and the like,--(B) Any underground or partly underground place of deposit for wine, provisions, fuel, or the like. In cities there is often a special chute for coal, kindling wood, and the like; and the cellars of stores and warehouses have elevators or lifts, often outside the walls of the building and in areas.

Cement, Calcareous: A cement consisting largely of lime, the other ingredients being chiefly clay, which gives to such cement a greater or less degree of hydraulic ability. (See Hydraulic Cement) It may be either a natural cement,--that is, prepared directly from one of many natural forms of impure limestone,--as is the common Rosendale cement extensively used in the eastern United States; or artificial,--that is, prepared by mixing limestone or chalk in certain proportions with clay and perhaps a small amount of other ingredients,--as Portland cement. Such elements are supplied in the form of a fine powder, and require only to be mixed with water and sand for use as mortar, although a certain proportion of common lime is frequently introduced, usually for reasons of economy.

Cement, Hydraulic: A calcareous cement (see above) which has the property of setting under water without exposure to the air, and which is therefore valuable for subaqueous and similar masonry work. The hydraulic cements used in building are derived from the impure limestones, containing different proportions of clay and silica, or are artificial combinations of those materials with common lime, calcined and ground. The name "Roman cement" is applied in Europe to all the light, natural cements, the materials for which are found in great variety, and widely distributed. The stone generally contains about sixty per cent of lime and magnesia to about forty per cent of clay (silica and alumina), generally with a little iron and potash. The stone is burned in kilns until completely calcined, but care is taken that it is not overburned, which would render it inert. The Rosendale cements, among the best of those found in the United States, are of this class. They contain carbonate of magnesia in much greater proportion than the "Roman" cements of England and France. Others of this class are found in many parts of the United States,--in the valleys of the Potomac and James rivers, along the Erie Canal, in Ohio and Kentucky. With slight differences in composition, they posses nearly the same practical value. The Rosendales, from the valley of the Hudson, and the Louisville (Kentucky) are perhaps the best.

Cement, Maya: One composed of lime and zaccab.

Cement, Portland: An artificial calcareous cement composed primarily of limestone and clay. So called because of its resemblance, when finished with a smooth surface, as on the face of a wall, to the well-known Portland stone of England, where such cement was first manufactured. The Portland cements differ from the so called Roman cements in the relative proportions of lime and clay which they contain, the best proportions being 20 to 22 of clay and 70 to 80 of lime. They clay should contain about 1 1/2 or 2 parts of silica,

forming a silicate of calcium by the reaction of silica and lime in the presence of fusible combinations of iron and alumina. There is produced in the Portland cements a fusible silica-aluminate identical with that which forms the essential element of blast-furnace slag, in which sesquioxide or iron partially replaces the alumina. Its only useful purpose is to serve as a flux to favor, during the burning, the combination of silica and lime. When blast-furnace slags are precipitated, while still liquid, into cold water, they combine with hydrated lime in setting and give rise to silicate and aluminates of lime identical with those formed by entirely different reactions during the setting of Portland cement. These are the so-called "slag" cements. The various Portlands are made by mixing and grinding the material, generally wet, drying it, breaking it into pieces, and burning to incipient calcination. The weight of good Portland cement should be not less than 112 pounds to the bushel; that of the Roman and Rosendale cements is about 75 pounds.

Cement, Roman: See Hydraulic Cement.

Cement, Slate: (A) A hydraulic cement manufactured from argillaceous slate. (B) A plastic roofing material made of broken slate mixed with tar, asphalt, or some similar material.

Cement, Water: Same as Hydraulic Cement.

Cement: (A) To secure together by means of cement. (B) A plastic roofing material made of broken slate mixed with tar, asphalt, or some similar material. (C) Any material by means of which substances are made to adhere to each other. In this sense, glue is the cement most used in carpentry work; gum tragacanth, gum Arabic, and various mixtures are used under the general term mucilage for minor operations of the sort; shellac is much used in making small repairs in cut stone. Especially, in building, same as Calcareous Cement; also mortar made with a large share of that material.

Centering: A timber framework or mold, upon which the masonry of an arch or vault is supported until the key is placed which renders it self-supporting. The centering for a stone arch is composed of parallel frames or longitudinal ribs regularly spaced, which follow the form of the intrados of the arch, and upon them the transverse laggings are placed which support the stones of the arch. In small arches the laggings are planks forming a close surface; in larger works, each course of arch stones is supported by a single light timber. The ribs are formed sometimes of beams of convenient length, dressed on the outside to the curve of the arch, and supported at their ends, or junctions. For small arches they are formed of several thicknesses of boards cut to the proper curve and nailed together, breaking joints. The framing, or the supports of the ribs, vary according to the conditions and the skill of the designer. They may be divided into two general classes: those which are supported from the ground or floor under the arch by means of radial or normal struts, or by vertical posts; and those which are carried by the piers or abutments at the ends of the arch span, being either trussed or supported by arch braces transmitting the weight to the ends. The former method is much to be preferred when points of direct support can be obtained. The centering must be not only strong enough to carry the weight of the arch, but also so arranged that it will not change its shape as the successive weights are placed upon it. To facilitate this purpose in long spans, the masonry is sometimes placed on the arch in blocks, so that nothing is keyed or closed until the whole weight is on the center, and there is no risk of its changing its shape. At the Pont Notre Dame, in Paris, all the ring stones were laid dry, separated by small wedges; when all were in place the joints were filled with mortar with a fiche, or sword, with a notched blade made for the purpose.

Centrally Planned: A building planned to radiate from a central point in contrast to axial plan.

Cesspool: A sunk pit, generally covered, intended for the reception of solid and liquid waste matters, as from inhabited buildings. There are two kinds of cesspools, viz., leaching and tight cesspools; the former built of stones laid dry, with open sides and bottom, permitting the liquid sewage to escape or leach away into the subsoil; the latter built of stone or brickwork, laid in hydraulic cement mortar, and made water-tight in the same manner as cisterns. From a sanitary point of view cesspools are condemned as involving the storage on the premises of putrefying organic matter. Cesspools are often built in two chambers, the first being a settling tank for solids and retaining the greasy scum (grease trap); the second a liquid chamber, emptied by bailing out or pumping out when filled, and the two chambers being connected by an overflow pipe, dripping well down into the first chamber.

Chair Rail: A horizontal band or strip, generally of wood, secured to the sides of a room at a height from the floor equivalent to the usual height of the backs of chairs, in order to prevent them from injuring the face of the wall. It is commonly decoratively treated to conform with the general woodwork, and the space of wall beneath is often finished as a dado.

Chalet: A house built in the traditional Swiss style, originally a Swiss mountain cottage.

Chalking: Powdering of the paint film on the film surface. Mild chalking can be desirable however heavy chalking should be removed prior to repainting.

Chamfer: The bevel or oblique surface produced by the cutting away of a corner or arris. When the chamfer does not extend the whole length of the arris, it is called a stopped chamfer (see Stop). When instead of a bevel there is a concave surface replacing the arris, it is called a concave chamfer. A beaded chamfer is one in which a convex bead is left projecting from the bevel of the chamfer. A beaded chamfer is one in which a convex bead is left projecting from the bevel of the chamfer. Chamfers occur principally in woodwork, and occasionally in stone cutting.

Chancel, High: The central or principal part of a chancel in a large church where there are aisles or a deambulatory. The need of the term comes from the confusion between the use of "choir," "chancel," etc., to denote particular sacred enclosures, and the use of the same terms to denote the entire easterly division of the building.

Chancel: That portion of a church set apart for the use of the clergy, and where the Holy Eucharist is celebrated, and the divine office is chanted. It is situated at the rear, and therefore property eastward, of the nave, from which in large churches it is separated by a screen or rail, and, as its floor is higher than the nave, it is approached by one or more steps. The chancel is often divided into two parts, the choir and the sanctuary, separated by the altar rail. The division nearest the nave is the choir (the place of the singers), and the division east of the choir is the sanctuary (the place of the high altar), the place referred to by S. Ambrose (A.D. 397) in the following words addressed by him to the Emperor Theodosius, "The priests alone, O Emperor, are permitted to enter within the rail of the altar, retire (to the nave), then, and remain with the rest of the laity." The altar is in the center of the sanctuary; the credence (or the table for the bread and wine, the sacred vessels, and the missal) is on the south side; and near by in a wall recess is the piscina, a drain to receive the washing of the priest's hands and that of the sacred vessels. On the same side, but to the west, is a sedilia, divided into three seats, for the officiating clergy at the sacrifice; and on the north side, in the case of a cathedral church, the bishop's throne is now placed; anciently it was placed behind, and higher than, the altar. The term is, however, frequently used to denote the sanctuary only, as distinguished from the choir.

Channel: Any furrow or groove, whether for carrying off water or for any other purpose. A street gutter is in England is sometimes called a channel. In Greek Doric architecture it is applied to the grooves of the triglyphs and columns; those of the columns being called by this name to distinguish them from the flutes of the Ionic and Corinthian orders; though this distinction is not always maintained.

Chantry Chapel: A chapel within a church or attached to a church dedicated to the founder or those designated by the founder. Formerly used to celebrate mass in their honor.

Chapterhouse: The principal assembly place in a monastery. The chapterhouse is used for business purposes and connected to the cloisters, or living quarters.

Chase: A groove or channel formed in a structure, as in the face of a wall, to receive some accessory such as flues, wires, sliding weights, or the like. A chase may be left in a wall for the future joining to it of an abutting wall to be built later. A chase differs from a groove mainly in being relatively large, and in not

ordinarily calling for accurate fitting to whatever it is to receive.

Cheek: A narrow upright face forming the end or side of an architectural or structural member. Usually, one of two corresponding opposite faces, whether forming the sides of an opening, as the jambs of a doorway, or forming the two side faces of a projection, as a buttress or chimney breast. The term is often extended to mean an upright member or piece forming such a face, and this definition is accepted by the dictionaries, although the meaning given above appears to be the more accurate.

Chevet: The rounded end of a choir in a church, especially used in connection with the Gothic churches of France. The term includes the apse itself, or rounded end of the central part or nave, and also the aisle or aisles (see Deambulatory; Poutour) which pass around it.

Chime: A number of bells so proportioned to one another and so tuned that they are capable of being struck in harmony, producing a more or less elaborate piece of music. Chimes may consist of five, six, eight, or more bells; those consisting of many more being usually called Carillon.

Chimes are commonly played in one of three ways, viz.: 1st, by machinery with a revolving drum, the projecting bands upon which drum catch the ends of wires connecting with the clappers or hammers; 2d, by means of a keyboard, the keys of which connect in like manner with the clappers, and which can be played upon by the musician below; 3d, by pulling the bell ropes, one person having charge of each bell, and these ringers being trained to act in concert under the direction of a leader. It is held by persons who are students of the subject that only the swinging of the bells in this their manner, with their mouths uppermost, is properly

called chiming, or bell-ringing, all other devices being makeshifts.

In certain parts of England, the clergymen in charge of parish churches have of late years organized bands of their parishioners for the chiming of their church bells.

Chimney arch: The arch over the opening of a fireplace, supporting the breast. It is usually a flat or segmental arch.

Chimney bar: A bar or beam for the support or steadying of the masonry above a fireplace. It is eiter straight or curved, according to the form of the chimney arch, and is usually set a few inches back from the face of the arch.

Chimney-breast: The masonry structure projection into the room and housing the flue.

Chimney-piece: See mantelpiece.

Chimney-stack: Masonry containing one or more flues and projection above the room.

Chimney: That part of a building which contains a flue or flues for conveying smoke or the like to the outer air, and often encloses also the fireplace, if there is one; specifically, that portion which rises above the roof.

Chinking: (A) Material used for filling a hole or crack in a wall, especially in log cabins. Usually chips or sticks of wood. (B) The process or operation of filling small openings, or chinks, especially the interstices between the timbers of a log building, with chips, moss, clay, and the like. This operation is commonly followed by daubing, the entire process being known as chinking and daubing.

Choir Screen: Wood, metal or masonry partition separating the choir from the nave and transepts of a church. It is similar to the iconostasis in an Orthodox church.

Choir: (A) Primarily, that part of a church in which the singers were accommodated. In Catholic churches, where there were many persons employed to sing the Mass and other services of the Church, the space allowed for these singers and the clergy became very large; hence arose the signification B, which, however, is to be understood as inaccurate, and a loose term for that which has no accurate one. (B) In a church, that part of the main structure which is in great part occupied by the choir proper, A, above. This, in a cruciform church, will be that arm of the cross which is farthest from the main entrance; that is to say, at the east end of the church when oriented in the usual manner. Thus, in a large church, the term choir has two very different meanings: 1st, the actual enclosure in which the clergy and choristers perform their duty; and 2d, one great arm or extension of the building including the rounded apse, if there is one, and the deambulatory surrounding that apse, if there is one. The choir, being considered the most sacred part of the church, was often built in advance of the rest of the structure, and on this account many of the large churches of Europe have a choir of different date from the other parts. The floor of the choir is often raised higher than that of the nave. Where there is a crypt, this may occupy the whole space below the choir, the floor of which will then be much elevated; thus, at S. Zeno in Verona, the number of steps up to the choir floor and down to the crypt are about equal; and in S. Miniato al Monte, near Florence, the disposition is about the same, with sixteen rather steep steps leading up to the choir floor. In England, a similar arrangement exists in the cathedrals of Rochester and Canterbury.

Ciborium: A canopy suspended over a high altar in a church. Typically in the form of a dome resting on columns.

Cimborio: (Spanish) A lantern admitting light over a crossing tower or structure raised above a roof.

Cistern, Supply: A reservoir or cistern from which the water service of a house is wholly or partly drawn; it is generally excavated in the earth, lined with brick, stone, or cement, domed over at the top, and generally furnished with a chain pump, for aerating purposes.

Cistern: A structure or compartment for the reception and storage of water; built of brick or stone, or of wooden staves; one differently built being usually called a Tank. Cisterns are built underground of a round shape, except those of unusually large sizes, which are made square or rectangular. The size of a cistern is determined by the amount of rain water to be stored, and depends also on the area of the roof and the rainfall. To prevent contamination, cisterns are built perfectly watertight, and the inside, when of masonry, is plastered with Portland cement. The overflow pipe from a cistern must never connect with a house or street sewer, and is best carried into an open ditch or road gutter, the outfall being protected by a flapvalve, grating, or bar strainer. The top of such cistern is arched over and covered with iron or stone cover, and the surface graded away from same. Cisterns should be well ventilated, to prevent the water from becoming stagnant.

Citadel: A fort with four to six bastions. Usually connected to the outskirts of a town.

Cladding: The external skin of a structure applied for both aesthetics and protection.

Clamp: A piece or instrument for securing or holding, generally distinguished from other devices used for that purpose as being applied to the surface of the parts, and not passing through the material, although perhaps entering a short distance. It may be a member to unite two or more parts of a structure permanently together, as a cleat or strap; of a tool to hold temporarily one or more pieces of material in process of being prepared or finished, as a carpenter's screw clamp.

Clapper Bridge: A stone bridge which includes rough piers on which a roadway is built.

Clear: (A) Open, free of obstruction. (B) Clean, without impurities or defects; without admixture. Thus, clear cement is cement unmixed with sand or lime. (C) In connection with lumber, free from knots, shakes, sap, and the like. (D) Unobstructed space; opening considered as between the inside limits of two opposite parts. Chiefly used in the adjectival phase, in the clear, i.e. taken or measured at the narrowest part of an opening; in general, the shortest or perpendicular distance so taken.

Clearstory: That part of a building which rises above roofs of other parts, and which has windows in its walls. The term is especially used for medieval churches, whose division into a central nave and side aisles of less width and height made the opening up of the wider central nave a natural and obvious arrangement. It dates back, therefore, at least as far as the earliest Christian basilicas. A similar arrangement is, however, traceable in some buildings of Roman antiquity. The term, if used for such buildings, is used with a sense of extending the application of it beyond its usual meaning.

Cleat: (A) A strip of wood nailed, screwed, or otherwise fastened across a number of boards to hold them together or to stiffen or otherwise strengthen them; or secured to a wall or other upright as a support for a shelf, or the like. The cleat differs from the Batten generally in being smaller and in having only the significance of a piece used to secure together planks or boards laid edge to edge, or of stiffening a very wide piece of plank or board. The common term Batten Door would be better described as cleat door, for the transverse piece is short and need not be heavy; it may be thought, however, that the battens referred to in this term are the longitudinal or principal pieces. (B) A device for temporarily attaching a cord, as of an awning; usually of metal and consisting of a shank or short leg from which two arms extend in opposite directions. The cleat being secured in place by the shank, the cord may be wound about the arms.

Clocher: (French) A bell-tower.

Close: The plot of ground occupied by a cathedral and its dependent buildings, and formerly always enclosed by a wall. The closes of some English cathedrals are extensive, and contain fine trees of great age; the buildings also, being grouped in a picturesque fashion, give a parklike character to the whole.

Closet, Plate: In Great Britain, a closet or small room connected with the butler's offices for the custody of

plate. When the plate is of much value, such a closet is commonly made fireproof and is called a plate room or plate safe (Kerr). In the United States, usually a much less pretentious compartment called silver closet, silver safe.

Closet: (A) Originally, a private room; the sitting room or chamber of a person of some distinction. (B) In modern usage, a place for storage, distinguished from a cupboard only as being larger, perhaps large enough for a person to enter. By extension, the term covers such a small room when fitted with conveniences for washing, and the like, as a wash closet, a dressing closet.

Closure: A wall, balustrade, or arcade serving as a screen; but where standing at the edge of a roof, gallery, or the like, serving as a parapet. The term is especially used for a short length of such wall, etc., which is set between two columns, having usually no connection with the columns, but standing free.

Clustered Pier: See compound pier.

Coade Stone: An artificial cast stone invented in the eighteenth century.

Cock: A mechanical device for controlling the flow of water or other liquid, either at any point in the line of pipe (stop cock), or at an outlet end of a pipe line, in combination with a nozzle or discharge spout at a plumbing fixture (bibb cock, faucet). Cocks are designated by the fixture for which they are intended (as a basin or bath cock); by the service which they are intended to render; by their mechanical construction (ball cock, compression cock, three-way cock, ground key cock, self-closing cock); or by the fluid flowing through them (water, gas, steam cock).

Coffer Dam: A temporary dam made to exclude the water from a place upon which it is desired to build. In the usual form it is composed of an outer and an inner row of piles with waling pieces, or stringers, to guide and support the sheet piling which is driven between the piles of each row, forming a double enclosure. The space between the rows is then cleaned of all material not water-tight, and filled in with puddled clay and gravel to make the enclosure water-tight. It is sometimes made of large timber piles driven close together, jointed and caulked, and tied together with waling pieces. A bank of earth is sometimes sufficient in shallow water. The water is pumped out, and the construction proceeds.

Coliseum: The largest Roman amphitheatre known to us. It stands in Rome southeast of the Forum, in a flat which continues the valley in which the Forum is situated. Its exterior is well preserved for about four fifths of its perimeter, except that the fittings of the uppermost part are uncertain. It was built by Vespasian and his son and successor, Titus, at least as far as the top of the third story of the exterior, the solid wall with pilasters forming the fourth story having been added in the third century. (Also spelled colosseum.)

Collar-beam: A horizontal transverse timber connecting a pair of rafters between the apex and the wall-plate.

Colonnade: A number of columns arranged in order, usually in one line, and considered in connection with all the details of the order, and sometimes with the roof, pavement, stylobate, and other adjuncts. The term is usually limited to structures in which the columns carry an architrave, and excludes the arcade. When a colonnade is carried along three or four sides of the exterior of a building, or of a large court or garden, it is called a peristyle. When attached to a building to which it serves as entrance porch, it is called a portico; and this meaning is often extended to roofed colonnades of any description. Colonnades in Grecian architecture are peculiar in the placing of the corner column, as in the exteriors of Doric temples, at a smaller distance from the two neighboring columns than the other columns are from one another, this on account of the supposed need of greater effect of solidity at that point. The columns being all set somewhat out of the true vertical, the corner column is put the most out of plumb. The Grecian and Greco-Roman builders did not employ coupled columns; but this modification was introduced soon after the revival of classical architecture in the fifteenth century, and some of the most important architectural effects of the last four centuries have been produced by this arrangement; such as the great colonnade of the Louvre, built in the reign of Louis XIV.

Colossal Order: An order with multi-story columns.

Column, Attached: Same as Engaged Column.

Column, Clustered: Same as Clustered Pier; the term "column" in this sense is not accurate.

Column, Coupled: In plural, coupled columns; those set in a pair or in pairs. These may be in a continuous colonnade, as a peristyle or portico, and the disposition is then called Araeostyle.

Column, Demi: A column sunken halfway into a wall. Not a pilaster.

Column, Engaged: A round pilaster-like member, generally ornamental in character, without utility and most commonly built with the wall, or as part of the wall whose courses of stone are continued through the shaft. Even where the engaged column is a piece of costly and beautiful material, and is therefore not continuous with the structure of the wall, it is to be considered as a pilaster with a rounded horizontal section, rather than as a column.

Column, Knotted: A column, the shaft of which is shaped to appear as if tied in a knot, or as if composed of two ropelike parts interlacing.

Column, Lally: A column that is made of steel and filled with concrete and used on commercial and residential furniture.

Column, Manubial: Properly, a column decorated with spoils of the enemy; hence a triumphal or memorial column of any kind.

Column, Memorial: A structure having approximately te form of a column, with capital, shaft, and base complete, but having no heavy superstructure and erected independently as a memorial.

Column, Midwall: A column or the like which carries a part of a wall much thicker than its own diameter and which, therefore, stands about halfway between the face and the back of the wall, its axis being about the same as the axis of the wall. In some medieval styles, slender columns are seen carrying very thick walls which rest upon them, and this disposition greatly affects the general design.

Column, Mortuary: Among the American Indians of the Northwest Coast, a wooden column, or two together, set up to support a box containing either the ashes or the body of the dead. Sometimes this column was elaborately carved.

Column, Rostral: (A) The Columna Rostrata or pillar adorned with the beaks of ships, which stood in the Roman Forum, having been originally erected in commemoration of the victory of C. Dullius, 260 B.C. Other memorial and votive pillars of similar character were erected at different times, generally, as it appears, in commemoration of naval victories.

(B) In modern usage, a pillar in which sculptured representations or suggestions of beaks of ships are used as decorative additions; sometimes erected either along or in connection with other monuments in recognition of naval prowess.

Column, Symbolical: A column used to support a representative figure or emblem, as the columns of S. Mark in Venice and other cities of the ancient Venetian dominion; or to commemorate an event or person, as a rostral column, the column of Trajan, the column in the Place Vendome in Paris, etc.

Column, Trinity: A monument of slender and shaftlike proportions built triangular in plan, for at least a part of its height, as a specially sacred memorial. Several exist in Europe, but all of the seventeenth and eighteenth centuries, from which is appears that the fashion is of late origin.

Column, Triumphal: Same as Manubial Column.

Column, Unbending: A column of which the diameter is of such proportion to its height, that, under vertical pressure, it cannot be fractured transversely by any tendency to lateral bending. This proportion of safety varies according to the material used, a column of iron or steel being much more slender for a given service than one of stone or marble, which finds its idea of stability in the proportions of the Greek orders.

Column, Wreathed: A column so shaped as to present a twisted or spiral form.

Column: (A) A pillar or post; a pier rather slender than thick and especially one that carried a weight and acts as an upright supporting member. In this general sense, the word has been applied to the supporting parts of iron frames of all sorts; so that where the uprights of a piece of carpentry work would commonly be called posts, the cast-iron or wrought-iron uprights are called columns. (B) In special architectural sense, a supporting member of stone or some material used in close imitation of stone and composed of three parts, capital, shaft, and base; the shaft, moreover, being either cylindrical or approximately so,--that is, a many-sided prism, or a reeded or fluted body whose general shape is cylindrical. In this sense a column need not carry a weight at all large in proportion to its mass; thus the decorative use of columns for memorial purposes involves the placing of a statue, a bust, a globe, a vase, or similar object slight in proportion to the column itself as the only weight superimposed upon the capital. The term is still employed where some one of the above characteristics does not exist; thus, in the earliest columnar architecture,--that of the Egyptians,--there is no base, and the earliest columnar structures of the Greeks, namely those of the Doric order, were also without bases. Capital are, however, universal, and are to be considered as mainly decorative in character.

Columna Rostrata: An ornamental column decorated with ships' prows. From Roman architecture.

Common Brick: Ordinary bricks used for walls.

Compass, Bar: (A) A compass of which one leg can be lengthened by inserting a piece with sockets and screws between the joint and the point, for the purpose of drawing a circle or arc with larger radius. (B) Same as Beam Compass.

Compass, Beam: One for describing circles larger than are practicable with the ordinary jointed compass. The two legs of the compass are secured by clamped slides to a long, light, and rigid beam or bar of wood or metal. In the finer instruments, this is provided with a scale and the slides with verniers for accurate adjustment.

Compass, Bow: Small compasses having the legs held by a strong spring instead of a pivot, and adjustable to any span by a fine screw which compresses the spring. They are used for minute work for which ordinary compasses are too coarse or heavy. A complete set comprises bow-dividers or spacers, bow-pen, and bow-pencil.

Compass: (A) An instrument used in drawing and in the building trades for laying off, dividing, or measuring distances and for describing circles or arcs of circles. A pair of compasses of the ordinary type consists of two legs pivoted together at one end, and either pointed at the other (see Dividers) or provided with fixed or removable pencil, pen, and needle points for describing circles. For draughtsmen they are usually finely made of metal and commonly with steel points. Carpenters' and masons' compasses are much heavier, of steel or wood, and generally with an arc and thumbscrew for securing the legs at any angle. (B) Having in part, a circular form or outline; as compass-headed roof, one whose inner surface is that of a circular semicylinder, or nearly so; compass brick, a brick having one side shaped to a circular arc, as for building a curved wall.

Compasses; Three-Point or Triangular: Those having three legs by which three points can be laid off at once.

Component: (A) A constituent part, ingredient. (B) In codes, any assembly, subassembly, or combination of elements for use as a part of a building which may include structural, electrical, mechanical, plumbing and fire protection systems, and other building systems affecting life safety. (C) In mechanics, one of two or more forces which make up the force with which the constructor is concerned; or into which that force may be considered as being divided.

Thus, in estimating the force of wind against a sloping roof, that force may be considered as resolved into two components, viz. one acting normal to the roof and producing a transverse stress on the rafters, the other acting in the direction of the slope and tending to overturn the roof.

Composite Order: One of the five orders recognized by the neoclassic architects and described by the writers of the sixteenth century. In its original form it is a classical Roman adaption of the Corinthian order; one of very many modifications which that order received to make it still richer and more elaborate, especially in the ornamentation of the capitals. As described by the sixteenth century writers, the capital consists of volutes and ovolo between them, borrowed, with modifications, from the Ionic capital; and of the circle of acanthus leaves applied to the lower part of the bell as used in the Corinthian capital.

Composite: Composed or compounded of a number of elements, especially somewhat diverse elements, united or harmonized into a congruous whole; used chiefly of artistic design, the corresponding term compound being employed in structural science. Thus we say a composite capital, a compound truss. But composite is sometimes used in structural nomenclature with reference to the union of diverse materials, as timber and iron, in one construction.

Composition (compo): A decoration used on cabinets and substituted for carvings.

Composition: (A) In fine art, the act of arranging parts in a design; the term being equally applicable to color taken by itself, or to line taken by itself, or to masses of light and shade, or to all the elements of the work of art considered as making up the general result. Also, the act of making such arrangements in design. (B) A design, considered as the result of several or many parts or elements combined into one. (C) A material made up artificially and used in modeling decorative friezes, centerpieces, and the like; a general term used for plastic material of unknown or unspecified make.

Compound Pier: A pier with multiple shafts.

Compression Member; Piece: In a framework, truss, or the like, a Brace, a Post, or a Strut, which are the more specific terms for pieces calculated to resist strains of compression in the direction of their length. The term is not usually understood as applying to a piece of material which merely sustains a weight through its resistance to crushing, as a template.

Compression: Stress given to a body causing it to become shorter or smaller.

Conch: A semicircular niche surmounted by a half-dome.

Concrete Blocks: Blocks of concrete used in building that are either hollow or solid.

Concrete: A building material made by mixing small fragments of hard material with mortar, so as to form a kind of artificial stone. There are different ways of mixing, and also of applying it; thus, in good work, granite, trap rock, or other hard stone is broken into pieces with a given limit of size, as when it is specified that every fragment shall pass through a ring of 2 inches inside diameter but this precaution is often very improperly dispensed with. So in putting the concrete into place; it is sometimes mixed on the spot, shovelled into place, rammed, and left to harden; but formerly many English engineers have required that it should be thrown from a height into the trench or box which is to receive it, a defective method generally abandoned.

Concrete may be made in solid blocks, being rammed in a mold; and these may be used to build with even in the form of lintels, as, if made of good materials, it is capable of enduring a considerable transverse strain. It is most commonly used in the way of foundations by filling up trenches in the ground and so forming a level and permanent bed for the mason work above. Even in foundations laid upon solid rock, great use is made of concrete, by means of which the irregular broken surface left from the blasting or the pickaxe can be smoothed to a perfectly uniform bed capable of receiving the most carefully laid walling.

The concrete of today is made of broken stone or gravel, usually not more than 2 1/2" in any dimension, with a mortar the composition of which varies with the purpose of the work. If the natural light-burned cements are used in concrete for foundations not under water, and for the backing or hearting of heavy walls, two parts of sand to one of cement and five parts of broken stone and gravel is sufficient. For subaqueous work, for foundations, for walls much exposed to the weather, Portland cement only should be used, which will bear more sand and consequently more of the hard material; two and a half to three parts of sand may be mixed with one part of cement and five or six parts of broken stone and gravel. They are mixed preferably by machinery; if mixed by hand, the mortar is spread upon a solid bed, the stone or gravel placed upon it, and the whole turned over until each stone is coated with mortar. It is then transported to its place in the work, levelled in layers of 6 to 8 inches, and rammed until the fluid mortar appears upon the surface. The finer kinds of concrete, made with very small materials carefully mixed and molded, may be classed as artificial stone.

Conduit: (A) A channel or pipe for conveying water or other fluids. (B) A passage, underground or otherwise concealed, for secret communication. (C) A tube for protecting electric wires.

Confessio: A chamber in medieval churches under the altar housing a relic.

Construction, General: (A) The manner in which anything is composed or put together. (B) The act and the art of putting parts together to produce a whole. (C) A completed piece of work of a somewhat elaborate kind; especially a building in the ordinary sense.

Conurbation: A city planning term denoting a group of towns geographically or functionally linked together.

Cope: (A) To overhang with a downward slope, as the soffit of a corona. Generally, cope over. (B) To cover or finish with a coping. (C) To join so as to create two intersecting, correspondingly molded members,by shaping the end or butt of one piece to form a surface which shall be the reverse of, and fit closely against, the side of the other, so that the moldings appear to miter or return. Hence, to cut out or shape so as to cope.

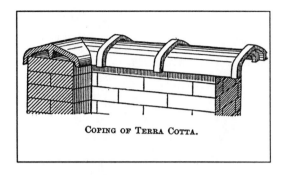

COPING OF TERRA COTTA.

Coping: Material or a member used to form a capping or finish at the top of a wall, pier, or the like to protect it by throwing off the water on one or both sides. In some cases a level coping suffices, if of stones or tiles wider than the walls; usually it is formed with a pitch one way or from the center both ways. The medieval architects gave great attention to their copings, especially on gable walls, which were commonly carried above the roof, and on balustrades and parapets, finishing them usually with a roll or astragal on top, a slope each way, sometimes in steps, and a throating or grooving on the under edge where it projected beyond the wall. Wooden or metal copings are employed over fences and in cheap construction.

Corbel Course: A projecting course of stones supporting horizontal members.

Corbel Table: A set of corbels below the eaves. Common in Norman architecture.

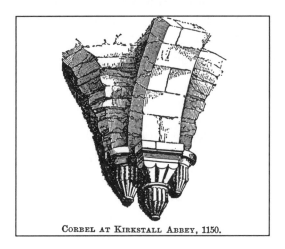

CORBEL AT KIRKSTALL ABBEY, 1150.

Corbel: A bracket of that form which is best fitted to ordinary conditions of cut stone or of other masonry; in French, the corresponding term corbeau is limited to a bracket having, particularly, two opposite vertical sides, as distinguished from the cul de lampe, which has a generally pyramidal or conical shape. In this limited sense a modillion is a corbel; but the term "corbel" is used more commonly for medieval and outlying styles of architecture. In English books the term has a special application to those wall brackets of many forms which in Gothic architecture serve as starting places for vaulting ribs. Sometimes these are simple culs de lampe; but sometimes they are dwarf vaulting shafts, with caps and bases.

Corbelling: Masonry course progressively extending out beyond the course below.

Corinthian Order: One of the five orders recognized by the Italian architects of the sixteenth century and described by the writers of that time. It is one of the three orders used by the Greeks, but its origin was late in the independent development of Greek architecture, and there are only a very few monuments of pre-Roman time in which it is known to have existed. Of these the most important is the circular building at Epidaurus. The little building in Athens known as the Choragic Monument of Lysicrates is another instance. This order was adopted by the Romans of the Empire as their favorite one for elaborate work, and in some of their monuments is treated with great beauty, even the buildings erected far away from the center of the empire retaining great charm of elaboration, as in Palmyra and Baalbek, in the palace at Spalato, the Maison Carree at Nimes, and, especially, at Athens in the temple of

Olympian Zeus, which was finished, and probably entirely built, under Hadrian.

Cornerstone: A carefully prepared and dressed stone which is put in place with certain ceremonies on a fixed day soon after the beginning of an important building. It is usual to select a prominent part of the building, such as one of its corners, and also to carry up the foundation walls to a little distance above the ground level of the site, in order that the stone, once laid by the officiant, may remain in place permanently. It is also common to prepare a small cavity in the stone to receive certain documents, as a description of the undertaking, a list of its promoters, a few newspapers of the day, some current coins, or other things, which are thus handed down to an uncertain posterity. Anciently, a stone of the actual foundation was treated in this way, and the term Foundation Stone (A.P.S.) was used to describe it.

Cornice; Block: In neoclassic architecture, a wall cornice produced by a simplification of the classic entablature. Modillions of some sort, usually very plain, carry a cornice proper of slight projection, and rest upon a simple bed Mold.

The term is used loosely for any very plain wall cornice.

Corona: The vertical projection at the top of a cornice.

Corps de Logis: (French) A main building as opposed to an out building.

Corridor: A passageway in a building, usually one of some size and importance, or belonging to a building of architectural pretensions.

Corridor Lobby: A wheelchair turnaround space in a corridor provided with seating.

Corrosion: The process of gradual decomposition or wearing away by chemical action, as by the action of water on iron, producing rust. Differing from disintegrating, which is the result of mechanical action. In practice, the term is generally used only in the case of metals, decay being the usual term in the case of stone or wood.

Corrugate: To form into alternate ridges and furrows (corrugations), as in preparing certain forms of sheet metal, wire lathing, etc., for use in building.

Corrugated Metal: Metal which in thin plates has been drawn or rolled into parallel ridges and furrows. The object or the corrugation is to give greater strength to the plates of metal to resist bending in the direction of the furrows, or perpendicular to the general plane of the sheet, also to permit expansion and contraction laterally.

Corrugated iron is used largely to cover roofs of buildings of a certain class, machine shops, car houses, barns, etc. The sides and ends of such buildings of the cheaper class are sometimes covered with it. The sheets of corrugated metal are supported on purlins to which they are attached by long hooks, or on sheathing where they are secured with long soft nails driven through and bent on the under side. All holes for nails, rivets, or clamps are made in the top part of a corrugation.

Counterpoise: A weight which tends to balance the action of another weight; in architecture, especially, a weight considerably greater than another and which prevents any injurious action by the latter. A corbel, for instance, acts by means of the heavy counterpoise which holds in place its longer and heavier member, generally built into the wall; and prevents the dislocation of the building by the weight acting upon the projecting part of the corbel.

In the ancient building of India, almost all of the most remarkable pieces of construction have been carried out by means of a system of counterpoise, as the arch is almost ignored, except in decorative architecture, and a system of corbels and braces resting upon them is at the bottom of all extensive and elaborate work.

Countersink: (A) To form a depression or hole for the reception of a piece or member which is not to project beyond the general surface. The cutting may be made to fit accurately the object, as in setting a hinge flush with the surrounding woodwork, or it may be a recess larger than the member, as a hole made to receive the head of a bolt. (B) To let into a surface by means of a recess as above described.

Couple: (A) A pair of forces equal, parallel, and acting in opposite directions, but not in the same straight line. They tend to make the body acted upon rotate about an axis upon which they exert no pressure.

(B) A pair of rafters with their tie beam, collar beam, or other pieces which go to make up the simplest form of truss. (C) To arrange, set or unite in pairs. The term is used in combination with a great variety of structural terms, and is generally self-explanatory.

Coupled columns are those which are united in pairs, the two columns of the pair being very close together, as in the arrangement called Araeosystyle. The arrangement is not known to have existed in antiquity, although the plates of Wood's Ruins of Baalbec and Palmyra show at least two instances of it. The conjectural restorations contained in those plates have not been absolutely verified. It is often thought that the first instance of it is the great colonnade of the Louvre which was built in the seventeenth century.

Coupled pilasters occur in the Palazzo Stoppani Caffarelli (Vidoni) and the Palazzo Chigi, in Rome, both of the sixteenth century.

Couple, Main: A pair of principals; one of several couples which support other subordinate rafters.

Course, Blocking: A parapet; usually a very plain wall like a range of stone blocks, used to replace a pierced parapet, a balustrade, or the like.

In some cases the blocking course is not a true parapet, because too low to serve in that capacity, or because the roof has been raised to the top of it. In this case it is a mere flat band above the wall cornice.

Course: (A) One , generally one of many horizontal or less frequently inclined, row of relatively small pieces, uniformly disposed and more or less connected, bonded, or united in one structure or member, as of bricks when laid in a wall, slates on a roof, and the like.

(B) To lay in courses, as masonry; to lay evenly and more or less regularly, approximating uniform and regular courses.

(C) To build in courses of masonry, as a wall or pier.

Court: An open area intimately connected with a building or buildings, as: (A) A yard surrounded or nearly surrounded by buildings and often intended to afford light to their interior windows. The court of a medieval strong castle, that of an Italian palazzo, and that of a modern collect or statehouse, are equally intended to give light to the buildings fronting upon it, and in many cases, the chief light must be drawn from within; whereas in a modern hotel on the continent of Europe the court has so long been considered an essential thing, and the habitues of such a hotel are so accustomed to treat the open space as a kind of sitting room in pleasant weather, where they take coffee and the like, that the open space is retained, although now commonly sheltered from the weather.

Houses in the Levant, in Northern Africa, and in Turkey, have commonly no windows on the exterior (at least in the lower story), but the court is surrounded by arcades, and the rooms, which are not usually large, receive their light from the doors and from small windows. Moreover, because of the need of privacy, while at the same time there is the fixed habit of sitting, eating, and sleeping in the open air, it is very usual in warm countries to build around an enclosed court; thus, the old houses of New Orleans are so arranged, and the buildings of Spanish America have in their courts the same convenience which the habitants of northern countries where the summer is shorter, find in the veranda. It is, however, hard to explain the avoidance of the court by people of Teutonic race, who even in the hottest parts of India use the veranda instead.

Probably the common use of the court is a reminiscence of times when violence was more usual and when the shelter of the outer walls was found necessary. (B) A larger and freer space enclosed by walls, but not encompassed by the principal buildings; as in a medieval castle, where there were inner and outer courts, some of which were not more enclosed than by the strong walls which served as their defence. (C) By extension, a high room surrounded by smaller and lower ones, or by rooms or galleries in several stories. Thus, in a building for temporary exhibition, a court is often a large area open to the topmost roof, and devoted altogether with its surrounding galleries to a special line of exhibits. (D) Anciently, a castle or manor house, or large country dwelling. From this use of the term is derived its frequent occurrence in the names of English dwellings, as in the well-known instance of Hampton Court.

Cove Ceiling: The upper side of a room which is so designed that coves, large in proportion to the extent of the ceiling, join the vertical wall with the flat part of the ceiling. In interiors of the eighteenth century the cove is often very large and

without strong horizontal markings, either on the wall side or on the ceiling, and is richly adorned with paintings and carved panels which are, therefore, displayed in a position relative to the eye of a person sitting or standing below, which makes them easy to see and enjoy.

Cove: (A) A surface of concave, more or less cylindrical, form, whether of a small molding or of a large structure, as a vault or cornice. (B) To construct with a cove or coves; to give the form of a cove to.

Coving: (A) That part of a structure which forms a coved projection beyond the parts below, as a concave, curved surface under the overhang of a projecting upper story; a cove or series of coves. (B) The curved or splayed jambs of a fireplace which narrows toward the back.

Cowl: A cap, hood, or like contrivance for covering and protecting the open top of a pipe, shaft, or other duct while permitting the free passage of air. It may be merely a bent over portion of the pipe or a more elaborate device, as a contrivance for improving the draught of a chimney; usually a metal tube or pipe nearly as large as the flue and arranged at top with a curve so as to bring the smoke out in a nearly horizontal direction. It is customary to make the curved tube separate, free to rotate, and fitted with a wind vane, so that it will turn easily and always present the convex or closed part of the curve to the force of the wind. The term is also applied to a similar contrivance at the top of a ventilating shaft.

Cramp: In masonry, a small metal member to secure together two adjoining parts or pieces. It is usually a short flat bar, having its two ends turned down at right angles and embedded in holes in the stones.

Crandall: In stone dressing, an axelike instrument used in finishing the softer stones. Its head consists of a number of movable steel points, secured side by side in a slot through the end of the handle.

Creasing: A course, or several courses, of tiles or bricks laid upon the top of a wall or chimney with a projection of an inch or two for each course over the one below, to throw off water. The coping, if there is one, comes above the creasing. A layer of slates or of metal over a projecting string course or window cap, serving as a flashing to prevent the infiltration of moisture, is also called a creasing. The term is little used in the United States.

Credence: (French) Sideboard. A table or shelf near an altar in a church to hold the elements of the Eucharist.

Crepidoma: The stepped base of a Greek temple.

Crescent: A concave row of houses.

Cricket: A piece of sloped roofing laid in an otherwise horizontal valley so as to produce one or more sloping valleys to throw off water which would otherwise be retained.

Thus, if a sloping roof is interrupted by a chimney standing squarely across the slope, a horizontal valley would naturally result along the upper side. It is therefore usual to construct there a small piece of roofing sloping laterally in one or both directions, so as to produce one or two diagonal valleys at its meeting with the main roof.

Crinkle-crankle Wall: A serpentine wall.

Cross, Archiepiscopal: One which, having the general character of the Latin cross, has two horizontal bars instead of one.

Cross, City: In the Middle Ages, a structure with a raised platform from which public addresses could be made, laws and edicts proclaimed, and the like; usually, a steeplelike ornamental building ending in a cross. In some instances, this structure was high and elaborate enough to supply a pulpit or stand for the speaker, raised above the pavement at the base.

Cross, Consecration: One used with others in the ceremony of consecrating a church. Such crosses were frequently made a part of the permanent interior decoration of a building.

Cross, Craddle: One on which the four arms are equal in length. It is customary to speak of churches whose nave, choir, and transept arms are equal, or approximately equal, in length as built on the plan of a Greek cross.

Cross, Greek: A cross with four equal arms.

Cross, Latin: One which has an upright much longer than the crossbar, or, in other words, which has three arms equal or nearly equal in length, and the fourth much longer. The ordinary Romanesque and Gothic church in Western Europe, and all the churches which succeeded the classical revival, and in which the nave is longer than the choir and much longer than either arm of the transept, is commonly spoken of as being built on the plan of a Latin cross.

Cross, Market: Same as City Cross; the term arising from the common usage of locating such crosses in the principal market place of a town.

Cross, Memorial: Any cross erected in memory of a person or event.

Many City Crosses, Preaching Crosses, and the like were originally memorial crosses.

Cross, Poultry: The Market Cross at Salisbury, Wiltshire, England.

Cross, Prayer: One erected in a village or at the crossing of important roads, or the like; generally, with a small altar at which mass could be said on certain occasions, and with a figure of Christ or a group of the Virgin and Child. A very few of these still exist, at least in part; one is mentioned as standing at Royal (Puy de Dome). A few of these were in bronze, and drawings of some have been preserved.

Cross, Preaching: A cross erected by the roadside, or in the market place of a town, generally upon a stone platform, approached by a few steps, called a Calvary, where monks or friars could address the people. It was generally a simple structure, the cross forming the finial of a stone shaft. In market places, however, the preaching cross was often a polygonal building richly decorated with an open vaulted story below, and a spire above with pinnacles and statues. Memorial crosses were,

on occasion at least, preaching crosses.

Cross, S. Andrew's: A saltire, that is a cross with four equal arms, but set diagonally.

Cross, Tau: An object having the form of a capital T, associated with certain early mysteries of faith which were perhaps derived from the Ankh.

Cross, Wayside: A cross erected by the side of a road in Roman Catholic countries as a station for prayer, or to commemorate a local event, as a murder or other tragedy.

Cross, Papal: A modification of the Latin Cross, having three horizontal arms.

Cross Bracing: (A) Any system of bracing with crossed struts or ties, as in many bridge trusses. (B) In house carpentry, the term is used specifically for continuous lines of crossed braces or struts between the floor joists, these lines of cross bracing being put in at intervals of 6 or 8 feet to stiffen the floors by distributing over several joists any shock or strain upon one. Generally called Bridging, Cross Bridging or Herringbone Bridging.

Cross Bridging: A kind of bridging consisting of a series of small diagonal braces set in rows transversely to the timbers. The braces are generally of light scantling, about 2 inches by 3 inches, or somewhat less, and, in floors, extend from the top of one beam to the bottom of the next, crossing each other at the middle. The term, as also herringbone bridging, is usual in the United States; drumming, twanging, strutting, and herringbone strutting being applied in different parts of Great Britain. The continuous rows of such crossing braces are generally put in about five or six feet apart.

Cross Rail: A primary horizontal member of a timber-from wall.

Crossing: The area at the intersection of the nave, transept and chancel of a church.

Crown-post: A vertical timber standing centrally on a tie-beam and supporting a collar purlin.

Crown: (A) The head of anything, especially of an arch or vault. Like Haunch , the term is applied to a part of an arch which cannot be limited exactly. By extension, used attributively, as crown cornice, crown molding, and the like.

(B) A decorative termination, as of a tower or turret, which is assumed to resemble a crown in the common sense, such as finished the well-known tower of S. Dunstan's church in the city of London. In this, the steeple is replaced by four flying buttresses each starting from a pinnacle and meeting in the middle; where they carry a small, very slender spire which rests entirely upon these open arches.

The church of S. Giles in Edinburgh, which dates from a much earlier time than the London tower, has eight arches springing from the four corners and the axes of the four faces of the tower, and these carry a laternlike steeple of considerable elaboration, the whole structure being a singularly effective piece of the very latest Gothic feeling lingering in the sixteenth century.

Crucks: Pairs of inclined timbers in timber-framing.

Crutch: In England, one of a pair of inclined timbers joined at the top and connected by one or two tie beams, the resulting frame forming the unit in the framework of early houses. Such pairs of crutches were placed at more or less regular distances apart, the included space being known as a bay.

Crypt: A vault for relics and burials in a church or cemetery. They may be below or above the ground or floor.

Cryptoporticus: An enclosed gallery with pierced walls rather than columns. Common in Roman architecture.

Crystal Palace: An exhibition building composed in large part of iron and glass; a popular term. The original one was that built in Hyde Park, London, for the great exhibition of 1851, the first international exhibition. The name was then extended to the great building at Sydenham, southwest of London, and, though less universally, to the New York exhibition building which stood at Sixth Avenue and Forty-second Street.

Cupola: (A) A bowl-shaped vault; and the imitation of such a vault in lighter materials. The significance of the term is in its form, and while it is erroneous to speak of a lath and plaster imitation of a Gothic roof as a vault, it is still correct to call a bowl-shaped roof a cupola even if it is hung from the roof timbers.

A distinction is then to be made between (1) those cupolas which are of solid construction as in the Pantheon at Rome, about 142 feet internal diameter; the cathedral at Florence, about 141 feet; the church of S. Peter at Rome, about 139 feet;

the ruined laconicum of the thermae of Caracalla, about 126 feet; the mosque of S. Sophia at Constantinople, about 100 feet; and the mausoleum of Sultan Mahmud at Bijapur in northern India, which appears to be 124 feet wide, and is built on such terms of construction as to make it a marvel of lightness. In all these cases the support of the cup-shaped vault, as by Pendentives or by a Drum, is of especial importance.

(2) Those cupolas which are partly of masonry; thus, the cathedral of S. Paul, in London, has the innermost curved ceiling, which is visible from the pavement, of solid masonry; and the haunches of this support a cone of brick which carries very sufficiently the lofty and elaborate stone lantern; but the rounded outer shell of the cupola is of wood and lead, resting upon the circular drum of stone and upon the brick cone. The Dome des Invalides in Paris, where now is the tomb of Napoleon I, built in a similar way of wood above two inner structures of stone, but having in this case a wooden lantern also. The church of the Val-de-Grace, in Paris; of beautiful contour, but similar in structure. The church of S. Mark at Venice, which has five masonry cupolas seen from within, the largest about 47 feet span, and each of these capped by a high outer shell of wood and metal.

(3) Those cupolas which are not of masonry in any part, but, if of any pretensions to size or permanence, usually of iron. Of these, the most interesting are those of the Halle au Ble at Paris Capitol at Washington; of great dimensions and built out in an ingenious way beyond and around the original drum of masonry, that of the Paris Exhibition of 1878, somewhat more than 100 feet in diameter, and an admirable piece of engineering, and that of the Paris Exhibition of 1889, nearly as large and very successful in design. There are also the cupolas of special character, such as those of wrought iron with the spaces filled in with tile which roof the reading-room of the Bibliotheque National at Paris. These are not large, having each only about 32 feet diameter, but nine of them are combined in one roof; the supports being four slender wrought iron columns, and twelve piers built into the outer walls of the room. In like manner, the later Byzantine style which constitutes a large part of Russian architecture,

have cupolas of which the drums are singularly lofty, and are pierced with elaborate systems of windows, while the cupola proper or rounded part becomes a mere roof to a tall cylindrical shaft. (B) In popular usage, a small structure built upon a roof either for a lookout or to complete a design. Such buildings are commonly of the nature of a lantern having windows on all sides, and being lightly built. In some cases, however, they protect the heads of winding staircases and are then more massive, with, perhaps, a single opening serving as doorway of exit to the roof.

Curb: A piece or series of pieces along the edge of a structure to protect, strengthen, or retain other parts or materials, especially when rising above an adjoining level. Specifically: (A) A dwarf wall or similar structure, acting more or less as a retaining wall; as the upper part of the wall surrounding a well and which projects above the ground: a well curb. (B) A line of vertical stones along the edge of a sidewalk, often called curbstone, or collectively, curbstones. (C) A retaining number or belt, forming a ring at the base of a dome, as an iron framework, or connected stones of a

course. (D) A similar horizontal member set between two successive slopes of a roof, retaining the feet of the upper ties of timbers; a coaming.

Curf: An incision, groove, or cut made by a saw or other cutting tool, especially one across the width of a board or molding, usually for the purpose of facilitating its being bent to a curve. Chimneys and piers which have leaned from the vertical are sometimes restored to verticality by cutting a curf in the side from which they lean.

In shaping a square timber from the log by hewing, it is common first to cut along one side of the log a series of curfs; that is, notches, the depth of which regulated so as to form a gauge for the subsequent cutting away of the wood between. (Written also Kerf.)

Curtail Step: The lowest step in a flight of stairs.

Curtail: In stair building, the outward curving portion of the hand rail and of the outer end of the lower step or steps of a flight; possibly an abbreviation of curved tail. An ample curtail to the lowest two or three steps not only enhances their appearance, but offers an easier start to persons approaching from the side. A plain semicircular curtail to the lowest step is called a bull nose.

Curtain Wall: A portion of wall contained between two advancing structures, such as wings, pavilions, bastions, or turrets. The term indicates position, and not character or function.

A curtain wall may be a mere screen, as to a court or yard, or a part of a facade; it may be solid or fenestrated, either higher or lower than its flanking structures, or of the same height.

In modern construction, most often a thin subordinate wall between two piers or other supporting members; the curtain being primarily a filling and having no share--or but little--in the support of other portions of the structure. Thus, in skeleton construction, curtain walls are built between each two encased columns and usually on a girder at each floor level or thereabouts.

Curve: In architectural drawing, a thin piece of wood, metal, hard rubber, or like material, cut to an outline of varied curvature for laying out, in a drawing, curves not

to be produced with the ordinary forms of compasses; either because they are not arcs of circles, or because they are circular arcs of very long radius. Sets of special curves are used in ship drafting and railway plotting; one or two pieces usually suffice for the architect, each having a considerable variety of curves in its outline. Sometimes called French curve and set curve.

Cushion: A frieze or part of a frieze projecting in a convex curve.

Cusp: In architecture, a point made by the intersection of two curved lines or members; especially in Gothic windows, tracery, etc., where the arch is diversified on its intrados by foliation, the curves of which are tangent to the inner edge of the larger arch. The simplest are those seen in the ordinary cusped arch. Gothic tracery affords many instances of the more elaborate sorts.

Cyclopean Masonry: Masonry in pre-classical Greek architecture made of irregular stones.

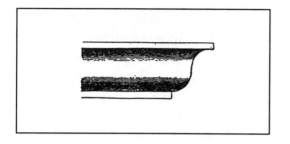

Cymatium: In classical architecture, the top member of a cornice in an entablature.

Cyma Recta: A fourteenth century molding in the shape of an *S*. Also called ogee molding.

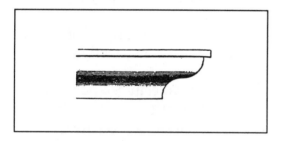

Cyma Reversa: A double curved molding, convex above and concave below. Also called reverse ogee molding.

CYMATIUM FROM A HOUSE NEAR SERDJILLA, SYRIA, C. 400 A.D.

D

Dado: (A) In Italian, a tessera or die; hence the flat face of a pedestal between the base and cap. In English it denotes a continuous pedestal or wainscot, including the base and cap molding, or sometimes only the plane surface between the base board and cap molding of such a continuous pedestal. A panelled wooden dado is generally called a wainscot; the words are often used erroneously as if synonymous. Dado is not usually used of an external pedestal course. (B) A groove formed by dadoing. Dado: A rectangular groove across the grain of a wood member into which the end of the joining member is inserted; also a housed joint: variations include "dado and tenon," and "stopped or blind dado" joints. (C) To cut or form with a groove or grooves of a rectangular section, as in making the upright sides of a bookcase which are so grooved to receive the ends of shelves. To insert in such a groove or grooves; to perform the whole operation of connecting parts in such a manner. Thus, it may be said of a bookcase that the shelves are to be dadoed in.

The term is usually applied only to such a method of connection when the groove is made to receive the full thickness of the inserted piece.

Dais: A speakers' platform at the end of a room. In medieval times the place the head of the house dined.

Dead Load: A more or less permanent and stationary load, as distinguished from the load of persons, movable furniture, and the like. Especially the load caused by the weight of a structure as distinguished from the load which it may be intended to support. Thus, in designing a truss or calculating the size of timbers to carry a floor, the weight of the flooring, ceiling, and other portions of the structure are considered as dead load.

Deafen: Properly, to render or to construct so as to be impervious to sound, as by the introduction of felt or other non-conducting material between the two thicknesses of a double floor, or by plaster filling between beams or studs. In this sense, same as Deaden. By extension, to fill in or construct in a manner similar to the operations described above, whether primarily for the purpose of preventing the passage of sound or not; as in making a floor fireproof by filling the spaces between the beams with non-combustible materials.

Deflection: The act of turning aside or the state of being turned aside from the normal form or direction; especially in building, the bending of a horizontal or other member as a beam or post under a load, or by the force of pressure, heat, or the like. Deflection may be temporary or permanent. Every member has a limit of safe deflection, which limit varies greatly according to the material. Thus, a stone lintel cannot be said to receive any perceptible deflection without rupture; but an iron or wooden beam may be deflected very considerably from the normal and yet be able to recover itself perfectly in case the load is removed; or it may carry that load with safety for a length of time.

Demolition: The operation of taking down a building by the gradual and systematic removal of its materials, as distinguished from destruction by fire, explosion, or the like. Demolition of old buildings requires care and system, and in cities must be carried on under special precautions against accident

and against public annoyance from dust, dirt, and falling materials.

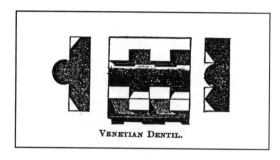

VENETIAN DENTIL.

Dentil, Venetian: One of a series of square blocks alternating with sloping surfaces. Also, the ornament so produced in general. A square-edged projecting fillet, or listel, is cut either on one edge or alternately on one and on the other side, so as to produce sloping surfaces which occupy half the width of the fillet. In this way a projection and a depression alternate along each cut side or edge of the fillet; the projections on one side of the double cut form, corresponding to the depressions on the other. The same form occurs, though rarely, in French Romanesque. There are other forms of square-edged ornament peculiar to Venetian architecture, some of which deserve the name dentil as well as the above-described form, but the term is generally limited as stated.

Dentil: A small rectangular block, forming one of a series closely set in a row, generally between two moldings, and intended for ornamental effect by alternation of light, shade, and shadow. Rows of dentils are found under the corona of an Ionic or Corinthian cornice. One of the earliest examples is in the cornice of the caryatid porch of the Erechtheum, Athens; another is that of the Choragic Monument of Lysicrates, while in Roman Ionic and even Roman Doric buildings it is a very common feature. In the Roman Corinthian, also, there is a row of dentils between two moldings under the modillions. The proportions of classic dentils vary considerably; in some of the best examples the width and projection are each equal to two thirds the height, and the inter-dentil or space is one third the height; which approximates to one sixth the lower diameter of the column. In Byzantine, especially Veneto-Byzantine architecture, a form of double alternating dentil is used.

Detail Drawing: A drawing showing the details of a composition, or parts of them. Such drawings are commonly made of full size, or on a scale two or three times greater than the general drawings.

Diameter: (A) An imaginary line through the center of a circle or sphere, and terminating in the perimeter or surface; a similar line in a circular cylinder. (B) The length of a diameter in sense A. In the system of proportions devised by the Italian architects of the classic revival (Vignola, Palladio, Scamozzi, etc.) for the classic orders, the diameter of the lower part of the shaft of a column was taken as a standard of dimension for all parts of the order. It was divided into two modules, and these into "parts" or minutes, twelve for the Tuscan and Doric, eighteen for the Ionic, Corinthian, and Composite orders. Other writers have used other subdivisions. This highly artificial analysis of the proportions, establishing a rigid and arbitrary canon, was evidently unknown to the Romans, although with their love of system they developed certain traditional rules, more or less flexible. Vitruvius gives certain of these, employing the term *crassitudo* for the diameter of the shaft as a unit for certain measurements and spacings; but he does not make it the basis of a whole system of detailed proportions as do the Italian classicists.

Diazo: A positive-to-positive reproduction process, rather than a positive- to-negative one like "blueprinting." It is a relatively dry process. Special machines are used to expose the "tracing" and a sensitive paper to ultra violet light. Then the sensitive copy is developed into a final copy. These *Diazo* copies come in blue line, brown and black line prints on bond paper, heavy "presentation" paper, or vellum (called Sepias). *Mylar* prints are also available. The prints are usually made on a white background. The clarity of the background depends on a high contrast between the lines drawn on the tracing and the vellum on which it is drawn. This is the reason you should make clear and dark lines in your original. Very light lettering guidelines and light blue colored pencil lines are virtually invisible to the *Diazo* machine and can be ignored when you prepare your tracing for reproduction.

Disintegration: The destruction of the cohesion of the particles of which a body is composed; especially as applied to stone. It is generally due to the destruction of the cementing

substance by the action of frost, or water, etc., as water which has been absorbed into the pores of the stone, in freezing expands and throws off grains and even scales from the surface. Like corrosion, disintegration can only be prevented by the application of a coating which will keep out the disintegrating force, generally freezing water, from the pores of the material. In some cases the action is chemical, as formerly in the smoke-laden atmosphere of London, that of sulphuric acid acting upon the carbonates of lime, etc. A coating of silicate of lime is efficient as a protection for some years. Various other substances and processes are on the market for this purpose, some of which are applied with heat. For works of importance, stones should be selected which are the least absorbent, in which the cohesion of the particles is most resistant, or whose chemical constituents are least liable to be injured by the gases to which they are to be exposed.

Dividers, Bisecting: Dividers so adjusted that the distances between two pairs of points have a constant ratio of one-half.

Dividers, Proportional: Dividers whose legs extend in both directions from the pivot, giving two pairs of points. The pivot is movable along a graduated scale so that the distances between the respective pairs of points may be adjusted to any given ratio. Thus, if it is desired to copy a given drawing on a scale twice as great, the pivot is placed on the graduated scale so that the distance spanned by one pair of points will always equal twice the amount subtended by the other pair. The scale is graduated mathematically for other proportions; and there is sometimes, also, a scale giving the ratios between the sides of regular polygons and the radii of their respective circumscribing circles, so that a given circumference may be readily divided into a desired number of equal parts.

Dividers: A pair of compasses having both legs terminating in points, for use in laying off given distances, or in dividing a given distance into a given number of equal parts; whence its name.

Dodecastyle: A portico with twelve frontal columns.

Dome, Gothic: A structure supposed to be possible or conceivable; at once a true cupola and Gothic in structure and design.

A true cupola could not exist in Gothic architecture. When, however, a vaulted compartment is much crowned-up, the rounded forms approach those of a dome in this sense.

Dome: (A) A building, generally one of importance, and a public building rather than a dwelling. The use, in Italian, of the word *duomo*, and the corresponding German word *dom*, applied to a cathedral church, seems to have had no influence in England. (B) A cupola; more commonly used for a large one covering in a good part of a building. In this sense also it is loose and inaccurate, and it would be far better if the word cupola were used exclusively for a roof of this kind. (C) An evenly curved vault on a circular base.

Domus: A single-family Roman house.

Door, window, and room finish schedules: Charts of blueprints that give information about doors, windows, etc.

Door, Hanger: A hanger for the support of a sliding door, especially such a door when hung from above. The meaning of the term is usually extended to mean the entire apparatus for such purpose, including the track or rails from which the door may be supported.

Door, Batten: One in which the body of the door is made of boards or planks having battens nailed across them to keep all in place; common in very rough work, barracks, sheds, outbuildings, etc.

Door, Blind: In the United States, a door having the character of, and serving as, a blind; i.e. having fixed or movable slats.

Door, Cellar: Any door, especially an outside door, leading to a cellar; more specifically, one set on a considerable slope with the vertical and often approaching more nearly to the horizontal; in use at the head of stairs leading to a cellar from outside the house. Low walls are carried up on either side of the stairway, and these slope from nothing, at the landing of the stairs, to a sufficient height above to correspond with the opening in the house wall, which itself must be high enough to allow head room.

Door, Crapaudine: A door turning upon a pivot at top and bottom, the pivots being let into sockets in the lintel and threshold.

Door, Doors, Royal: In Greek ecclesiology, those leading from the narthex into the church; sometimes the central door of three or five similarly placed.

Door, Doors, Weather: A door or pair of doors planned to shut quickly behind persons passing through the outer doors of a lobby, and so to prevent much ingress of cold air; these are commonly extra doors fixed outside of the usual entrance in cold weather, and the term is often used to include the light and sometimes temporary vestibule or porch which includes the door.

Door, Double Framed: One in which there is an outside framed structure complete with stiles and rails which encloses and holds a secondary framed structure of stiles, rails, and panels, the latter forming, as it were, a panel to the outside frame.

Door, Double Margin: A door made to appear as though consisting of two leaves, as in imitation of a folding door. It has a stile at the center twice as wide as the side stiles, and center beaded, or otherwise finished to resemble two stiles, therefore showing a double margin.

Door, Double: One which is divided into two folds, one of them being hung on each side of a doorway, the two folds, or valves, meeting in or near the middle, and closing the opening; commonly known as a Folding Door.

Door, Dutch: In the United States, a door divided horizontally into two pieces, so that the lower half can be kept shut, while the upper half remains open for the admission of air.

Door, Falling: Same as Flap Door, B.

Door, Flap: (A) A door placed horizontally or on an incline, and opening up, as is common, over steps leading to a cellar from the street. (B) A small door or shutter in a vertical opening, but hinged at the bottom so as to open downwards.

Door, Folding: A door divided into two or more folds, or valves, which are hinged to the frame or to one another. A few doors exist in which

each half is again halved, much on the principle of the folding inside shutters of a window. Of similar character are the doors arranged in schoolhouses, church lecture rooms, and the like, which, by means of a series of valves hinged one to another, may divide a large room as if by a partition, and open it up again into one room by folding against the wall the valves forming the partition. Something similar is to be found in connection with certain park gates which are closed by night and opened by day. In such cases, it is essential that the valves should be supported by means of little wheels running on arcs of metal set in the floor or the road. The above are properly folding doors, or gates; the word is applied also to Double Doors.

Door, Half: (A) Properly, one half of a Dutch Door; the term is also applied to the Dutch door complete, as when it is said that the outer doorways of a frame house are hung with half doors. (B) In the United States, a door less in height than the doorway, so as to leave a considerable opening above and below.

Door, Jib: A door so hinged as to be flush with the wall on either side, and to be, if carefully adjusted, almost indistinguishable when shut. The object of it is usually not secrecy, but the preservation of perfect symmetry in a room where other doors correspond each to each, and no such feature is desired at the place where the jib door is put.

Door, Ledged: One constructed with the use of ledges, as in a Batten Door.

Door, Overhung: One hinged at the top and swinging upward, requiring to be held open by a hook.

Door, Revolving: A weather door devised in the United States, which, when in operation, consists of four equal flaps hung at right angles to a pivot at the axis of a cylindrical structure within which the doors revolve. The outer edges of the doors are finished with rubber strips maintaining close contact with the inside face of the cylindrical shell, which is pierced with two opposite doorways so disposed that the direct passage between them is at all times closed by the doors, in whatever position. Pedestrians pass by pushing any one flap, as in a turnstile. When not in operation, the doors may be folded together so as to allow of direct passage at either

side, or bolted across the passage for security.

Door, Rolling: A rolling shutter applied to a doorway.

Door, Sash: One of which the upper half, or thereabouts, is constructed as a sash to hold glass; generally as one piece, but sometimes having a movable sash.

Door, Sham: A door finished only on one side, and set in a wall or partition to appear like a practicable door.

Door, Sliding: A door arranged so as to slide sidewise. In stables, freight houses, etc., it slides in the open against the back face of the wall; in dwelling houses it slides into a pocket in the wall or partition. It may be either single or double.

Door, Swing: One which has no striking piece, and swings past the door post at the side opposite the hinges. Such doors are commonly hung with double action spring hinges; but it is easy to arrange one with two pairs of single action hinges by using a strip of wood as thick as the door, hinged to the doorpost on one side and to the door on the other, the hinges being naturally turned in the opposite ways.

Door, Trap: One fitted to an opening in a horizontal, or nearly horizontal, surface, as a floor or roof, the essential fact being that a person ascends head first through it and descends feet first. The cellar door, as described above, is a variety of trap door.

Door, Venetian: A doorway divided into three parts by two mullions, or shafts, the central and wider part being occupied by the door, and the narrow side openings being windows. The central opening generally has a glazed arch over the door.

Door, Flush: A door that is level with framework and flush.

Door: The filling, usually solid, of a doorway, so secured as to be easily opened and shut. It is much more common to support a door by hinges secured to the doorpost or frame at the side; but a door may turn on pivots at top and bottom, as frequently in antiquity, or may slide or roll up horizontally or vertically. Where the solid filling is hung by hinges at the top of the doorway, or where it slides vertically, in the manner of a portcullis, it is rarely called a door. The doors of antiquity are but little known to us; a few of bronze, belonging to the later years of the Roman Empire, still exist, and it may be said that modern doors of metal have been studied from the ancient examples. The doors of the Middle Ages were usually of solid planks set edge to edge, and secured to each other by dowels or bands; the whole being held in place by the long strip hinges having holes through which nails were driven through the wood and clinched on the other side. Panel doors are not very ancient, but their obvious superiority in lightness, in permanent retention of their plane surfaces, and in counteracting almost entirely the shrinkage of wood, has made their use almost universal. Doors have always been a favorite medium for rich ornamentation.

Doors, Holy: In Greek ecclesiology, the doors of the Iconostasis.

Doors, French: Two doors that are joined together and open in the middle and have glass panes.

Doorstep: (A) The sill of a doorway; that upon which one steps in passing from a lower level through the doorway. (B) By extension, the platform with two or three steps outside of an outer door.

Doorway, Notched: A doorway narrow at the bottom for about one third of the total height, and then notched back to about double its starting width, on one or on both sides. It is found in the modern Pueblo Indian villages of Arizona, and in Cliff Dwellings and other ruins of the Southwest. In the Cavate Lodge construction of the Verde region in Arizona, another form occurs, as of a pear with the small end down, instead of rectangular. Doorways of this kind were adapted to Indian life, where burdens were carried on the back, making width at the bottom unnecessary; enough for the free movement of the legs being sufficient. As these openings were closed by blankets or mats, the narrow bottom part was an advantage in keeping out the winter air.

Doorway: An opening for entrance and exit from a building or part of a building; such an opening, together with its immediate surroundings.

Doric Order: (A) One of the orders of architecture containing twenty flutes and a column without a base.

(B) One of the five orders recognized by the Italian writers of the sixteenth century, to whom, however, Greek architecture was almost wholly unknown. (C) The style of architecture used in the greater number of Greek temples known to us, and of which the Parthenon serves as the type.

Dosseret: (French) A high block set on top of an abacus and placed between it and the spandrel of the arch above.

Double Hung: (A) Furnished with, or made up of, two sashes one above the other, arranged to slide vertically past each other; said of a window. Old houses, both in America and in England, often have only one of the two sashes hung with weights; the other being fixed, or, if movable, held in place by means of a button or prop; such may be said to be single hung. (B) Hung on both sides with cord and pulley; said only of vertical sliding sash. In some cases, where windows are narrow, or are divided by mullions into narrow lights, a window box with cord, pulley, and weight is furnished on one side only, the other side of the sash being sometimes fitted with rollers to facilitate its movement. Such sash may be said to be single hung.

Dovetail, Lap: A dovetail for joining two boards, as at a corner, in which part of the thickness of one board overlaps the end of the other. Thus, the dovetail of the overlapping board is formed, as it were, in the angle of a rebate which receives the end of the other board. It is frequently formed as a Secret Dovetail.

Dovetail: (A) Any piece or member having two flaring sides or edges, giving more or less a wedge shape, similar to that of the spread tail of a pigeon; especially a member, tenon, tongue, or the like, having such a form, and intended to fit a corresponding mortise or recess. This form of framing is especially adapted to unite parts subject to a tensile strain, the tongue being made to flare in the direction opposite to the applied force; as to unite the front and sides of a box or drawer to prevent their separation under the influence of a pull applied to the front. In masonry, the device is limited to cut stone as used in some elaborate constructions, such as fortress walls or sea walls. The celebrated Eddystone Lighthouse of 1759 had the lower part of the tower solid, and built wholly of joggled and dovetailed stones. (B) To cut

into the form of a dovetail or dovetails; to unite by means of dovetails and corresponding recesses, or the like. Hence, to unite, as at the corners of a box, or the like, by means of any similar series of tongues and slots, whether shaped like dovetails or not.

Dowel: (A) A pin, or similar projecting member, to connect two parts together. It may be formed on one of the two parts to be united and fitted to an aperture in the other; or, more commonly, a separate member, as a short rod, or the like, inserted part way into each piece. (B) Wood peg or metal screw used to strengthen a wood joint. Also see cramp.

Drafting Paper: Two kinds are used extensively in interior design drafting. The first is roll tracing paper that comes in white and yellow, and in various widths--18" is recommended. This is inexpensive and is used for under- and over-lays, layouts and sketching. The second type is 16 or 20 lb., 100% rag drafting vellum for finished work. This comes in plain and pre-bordered in many sizes--18" x 24" and 24" x 30" are the most common. The pre-bordered kind with end title blocks are the most common for architecture and interior design. The type with blue grids is most commonly used for engineering. It is usually divided into 10ths or 8ths.

Drafting tape: Tape similar to masking tape but not as sticky. It is used to hold tracing paper to the drafting board without damaging the paper or the drawing surface. Drafting tape is also less likely to leave gum on the paper and drafting board. 3/4" wide tape is the best all-around size.

Draftsman: One more or less skilled in drafting; specifically, one whose business it is to draw and prepare plans and designs, as for an architect. Also written Draughtsman.

Drain: An open or covered (underground) channel or pipe for the conveyance or removal of water or sewage. Drains are usually circular and made of earthenware, porous or unglazed, as well as glazed or vitrified. The term "house drain" is, in the New York Building Law, defined as "that part of the main horizontal drain and its branches inside the walls of the building, and extending to the connecting with the (outside) house sewer." Inasmuch as the term "to drain" means to draw off gradually, to remove by degrees, it would be more correct to restrict the term drain to pipes receiving subsoil water, and to call the pipes removing sewage from houses "sewers."

Drawing Inks: Inks that have a reasonable degree of permanence if kept from sunlight or strong diffused light. Shellac is the usual water-proofing ingredient, therefore it is necessary to thoroughly clean pens, instruments and brushes after use. To dilute black ink, add pure water with four drops of equal ammonia to the ounce. Tap water will suffice for washes which are applied at once. To dilute colored inks, use pure water only. Never add any acid or mix ink brands.

Dress Circle: Originally, in British theaters, the first balcony containing the boxes, and set apart for the wealthier class of the audience, who were supposed to appear in evening dress. It usually extended around three sides of the auditorium, the pit being either enclosed by it, or extending under it. In modern times, the term is used more or less indiscriminately to mean a similar part of a theater either on the main floor, or on a balcony above the orchestra, and next in importance to the latter, and most often without boxes.

Dress: To prepare, shape, or finish by cutting or rubbing one or more faces of stone, brick, or lumber; to face. (A) Brick is commonly dressed by roughly chipping to the required form, and then rubbing on a smooth surface with sand and water. When required to be more elaborately shaped or molded, the dressing is done by chisels and similar cutting tools in the same manner as stone. These processes are being largely superseded by bricks which are manufactured in a great variety of stock patterns, or by machinery with which bricks of the usual type may be readily and cheaply cut or ground, as for voussoirs. Where only a few bricks are needed, of an elaborate shape, they may be had cheaper by dressing than by molding. (B) Lumber is said to be dressed when planed on one or more faces, and is described or specified according to the number of sides which are to be so finished. At the present time, the greater part of such dressing is almost always done by means of machinery in planing mills, hand working being resorted to for small quantities, or to give a more perfect and true finish in parts left somewhat inaccurate and irregular by mill planing. Planing, whether by hand or machinery, commonly includes, not merely the dressing of lumber so as to form true and smooth faces and arrises, but also molding, either for decoration or for constructive reasons, and such molding is wholly or in part produced in one operation with the simple planing. Thus, floor boards are commonly manufactured as a stock article, planed on one side, and the edges tongued and grooved, while sheathing and ceiling is to be had finished in a similar manner, and also beaded on one or both edges of the face, or ever more elaborately molded. (C) Stone dressing, while commonly performed by machinery, is more often worked by hand than either brick or wood; first, because of the uneven texture of many kinds of stone, the slow, manual process of chipping is the only available means of dressing; second, because seldom used in pieces long enough to make planing or molding by machinery expedient; third, because many kinds of surface finish called for are very irregular in character. A combined process of dressing is, however, being rapidly introduced, in which a hammer, punch, or other tool is driven and caused to strike rapidly by mechanical means, while it is guided by the workman, who can thus, with very little labor, work moldings, and even produce elaborately sculptured forms.

Dressing: (A) In general, any one of the decorative furnishings, such as moldings, keystones, groins, and the like, projecting from the general surface of a building. (B) In a more restricted sense, the molded finish or framework around openings; as, for example, the architraves of doors and windows. This is the more common usage in England.

Dressings: Stones with a smooth or molded finished face, used around a window or angle.

Drill: A punch or boring instrument operated mechanically to drive holes through any hard material, as rock or metal, either by being rapidly rotated or by being caused to give blows.

Drip: Any projecting piece of material, member, or part of a member, shaped or placed so as to throw off water and prevent its running or trickling back to the wall or other surface of part.

Dripstone: A drip molding or hood mold to an arch, especially in Gothic architecture. The term is only applicable to exterior architecture; when such a molding occurs in interior work, it should be called a hood mold. Its section is convex externally, retreating to the wall by bevels and deep hollows. The term is sometimes erroneously used of the ornament at the ends of the molding, which is properly the boss.

Drop: The lower projecting end of a newel.

Drum: (A) One of the nearly cylindrical pieces of which a shaft of a column is built up when it is not a monolith. (B) The vertical wall, circular or polygonal in plan, which carries the rounded part of a cupola; called also Tambour. The drum applies chiefly to the exterior of buildings; thus, in the Pantheon or in the church of Hagia Sophia there is no drum; the cathedral of Florence has a very high octagonal drum pierced with an occulus in each face; and S. Paul's in London has a very lofty drum, which may be considered as having three parts, a plain basement, a lofty peristyle crowned by a parapet and surrounding a sloping circular wall pierced with windows, and an attic, which last carried the cupola itself.

Dry-wall Construction: Masonite used instead of expensive plaster.

Dry: In masonry, built without the use of mortar or any cementing material.

Dumbwaiter: A small elevator used to transport food or items other than passengers.

Dwarf Gallery: A wall-passage on the outside of a building contained by arcading. Common in Northern and Southern Romanesque architecture.

E

Eagle: (A) A pediment of a Greek building; the rarely used translation of oetos. Also the tympanum or recessed panel of such a pediment. (B) A reading desk or lectern, especially that used by an officiant in a church; properly applied only to one which has the form of a bird. Such eagles of brass, etc. were common in the Middle Ages.

Earthwork: (A) Work done in removing earth, gravel, loose stone, and the like. (B) With the article, a mound, rampart, or the like; used especially in fortification.

Easement: (A) A curve formed at the juncture of two members, to one or both of which it is tangent, and which would otherwise meet at an awkward angle; as where the sloping portion of a hand rail meets the horizontal part, or where a sloping hand rail is curved to meet a newel perpendicularly. (B) The right of accomodation, for a specific purpose, of another's property such as air or water.

EAVES OF A HOUSE IN SARAGOSSA, SPAIN.
The corbels, each of two horizontal timbers, carry a plate which supports the rafters.

Eaves: The lower portion of a sloping projecting beyond the walls, and forming an overhanging drip for water.

Echal: The enclosure of the Ark in a synagogue.

Elastic Limit: The limit of stress up to which the material takes no permanent deformation, or from which, being stretched or bent, it returns to its original form when the stress is removed.

Elasticity: (A) The power possessed by solid bodies or regaining their form after deformation which has not been so great as to overpass their limit of elasticity. When an ivory ball rebounds after falling on a hard surface it is because the ball seeks to regain its perfectly spherical shape, and the surface, as of a billiard table, also seeks to return from the compression which it has undergone under the blow. Ivory has much elasticity, marble somewhat less; many stones are very elastic, those which are the hardest, the most so as a general thing; but wood is of limited elasticity, and a bar of it is rather easily bent in such a way that it will remain bent, different woods differing greatly in this respect. On the other hand it has some elasticity, and notable instances of this may be named; thus, two heavy beams of hard pine supported a floor of artificial stone, and when the material of the flooring was still wet, yielded under its weight nearly 2 ¾" in the middle; but returned to an apparently perfect level as the floor dried, thus lifting the whole weight of this floor by their elasticity. Iron beams have much elasticity, as is evident from the peculiar vibration which a floor composed of them so frequently undergoes. (B) By extension, and inaccurately, flexibility or the power of adapting itself to irregular pressures and strains, said of a building or part of a building. It is customary to say of the Gothic construction, that it is elastic; by which is meant that it is capable of yielding a little without showing dangerous cracks, or without risking its solidity and permanence. There is also conveyed in this descriptive form an idea of that resistance of force by force which is peculiar to Gothic building. In this, the thrust of one arch is taken up or neutralized by the thrust of another arch, and so on until the last arch of a series thrusts against a flying buttress, which transmits the thrust finally to a solid and passive mass of masonry, the outer buttress, or to the foundations or the ground. In Roman Imperial and some other arcuated styles, there is little of this neutralization of one active force by another, but all arches have their thrust taken up by solid masses of masonry.

Elbow: In general, any relatively small piece or part of a structure bent or formed to an angle, as a pipe, an angle formed by two surfaces, or the like. Specifically:--(A) In English usage, (1) a short return or sharp angular change of direction for a short distance, in a wall, as for a recess; (2) in joinery, that portion of the jamb of a recessed window between the floor and bottom of the shutter boxing. (B) A piece of pipe formed either by a curve or by a miter joint to connect two sections of pipe at an angle. (C) The ear or projecting portion of a crossette to a door--or window--architrave.

Elevator, Screw: One of the earliest forms of elevator, in which the cage is raised or depressed by the direct action of a screw. In later elevators the principle of the screw is more scientifically applied in the form of a worm gearing, acting on the drum of the elevator machine.

Elevator: (A) A car or platform to convey persons or articles up or down to the various floors of a building. It may be raised and lowered by hand, steam, hydraulic, pneumatic, or electrical power, or by the force of gravity acting on weights. An elevator generally moves vertically, but may be arranged to run on an incline. Small elevators for conveying dishes and other small household articles are commonly known as dumb-waiters, and these are usually operated by hand. Large hand elevators are commonly known as hoists or hand hoists. (B) An apparatus for raising merchandise of any kind, such as grain in bulk; and, by extension and more commonly, a building containing many grain lifters and

large bins for the storage of the grain.

Ell: A North American term for a single-story kitchen wing attached to a residence.

Embankment: A banking or building of a dyke, pier, causeway, or similar solid mass; hence, by extension, the result of such work, especially in the form of a waterside street. The term is used to translate foreign words, such as the Italian and Venetian *riva, fondamenta*, and *molo*; also, for the French *quai*, for which the English quay is not always an adequate translation.

Embrasure: (A) A window or door recess in a wall of a fortified building. (B) An enlargement of a door or window opening, at the inside face of the wall, by means of splayed sides. Especially, in military construction, such an enlargement designed to afford a more extended range of vision from the inside by means of the sloping sides, while not increasing the outside opening. Hence,--(C) In military architecture, any opening through, or depression at the top of, a wall or parapet for discharging missiles; as a loophole, crenelle, or the like, because usually so splayed.

Enceinte: The main enclosure of a fortress.

Entasis: An intentional swelling in a column.

Entry: Originally, that part of a building by which access was had to its interior. Used indifferently for the doorway itself, the passage to which it leads, the outer porch, or all together. Later:--(A) In England, an alley or unimportant street leading to another street or public place. (B) In the United States, a passage in a house; more usually the principal passage leading from the front door, but frequently any passage, and even a staircase hall.

Equilibrium: The state of repose of a body under the application of forces which mutually counteract each other.

Escape: A doorway or a passage, private stairway, or the like, or all together; the object being to afford private exit, or a means of unobserved exit.

Eustyle: An arrangement of columns two and a quarter diameters apart.

Exedra: A semicircular or rectangular recess with seats. A niche at the end of a room and opening onto a larger space.

Exit: A gateway or doorway intended to serve only for persons leaving a building or enclosure, especially when prepared for use when a great crowd is dispersing. In some public buildings, such as theaters, there are exits for ordinary communications and others especially prepared for use in case of alarm.

Expansion: The act of growing larger and the condition of being enlarged, especially as caused under the influence of heat. All bodies possess the property of being expanded by heat, but in different degrees.

Extension: (A) A building added to another for the purpose of enlarging it; though this may be a peculiar way, and have a special purpose. Thus, a conservatory may be an extension to a house which has not had such an appendage before. hence,--(B) In local usage, probable only in the United States, a relatively small portion of a building, projecting from the main building, even if erected at the same time.

Extrados: The outer face of an arch or vault.

Eyelet: A small opening for light and air, or for the discharge of missiles, in the wall or parapet of a medieval castle; usually widening toward the interior, or backed by an embrasure. The opening was usually round or square, or else extremely long and narrow; sometimes with a cross slit, or enlarged at the center or ends by a round aperture for the discharge of firearms.

F

FAÇADE: CATHEDRAL, CREMONA; NORTH TRANSEPT.
This, having no intimate connection with the side walls, is essentially a façade.

Facade: The architectural front of a building; not necessarily the principal front, but any face or presentation of a structure which is nearly in one plane, and is treated in the main as a single vertical wall with but minor modifications. Thus, if a large building presents toward one street a front consisting of the ends of two projecting wings with a low wall between them enclosing a courtyard, that would be hardly a facade, but rather two facades of the two pavilions. With buildings which present on all sides fronts of similar or equivalent elaborateness of treatment, it is, perhaps, incorrect to speak of a facade; thus, in a great church, although the west front may be described by this term, it is inaccurate because that front would not be what it is were it presented without the flanks or north and south sides. The facade rather comes of street architecture and of buildings which have but one front considered of sufficient importance to receive architectural treatment.

Face: The surface of masonry or a wall that is exposed.

Facing: Finish applied to the exterior of a building. Materials such as wood, glass or stone that are put onto the outer surface of a building.

False Bearing: In English usage, a bearing or point of support which is not vertically over the supporting structure below, as that which is afforded by a projecting corbel or cantilever.

Fanlight: A semi-circular window over a door, common in Georgian and Regency architecture.

Fascia: A nailed board, under the eaves of a building, used for facing. A plain horizontal band in an architrave.

Faucet: A tube or hollow plug to facilitate the discharge or passage of water or other fluid, and fitted with some contrivance by which the flow is controlled. More specifically, in plumbing, a contrivance for allowing the outward flow of water and stopping it at will, this being usually a fixture at the end of a supply pipe for hot or cold water. Waterspouts so small as to be evidently intended for faucets, and wrought into very beautiful representations of lions' heads, dogs' heads, and the like, are found among Roman remains. These are usually of bronze. In modern decorative art, where the fittings of the bathroom or dressing room are to be made especially elegant, silver, plain or oxidized, and silver gilt have been used, the modeling being by sculptors of ability. These last are wholly exceptional, because modern plumbing appliances are made with sufficient accuracy and completeness of finish in great quantities and at a low price. In British usage, a tap.

Faux: A French term for something that is an imitation, such as simulated wood or marble.

Fenestration: The arrangement of windows in a building.

Feretory: A reliquary designed to be carried in a procession.

Fielded Panel: A panel with a plain raised central area.

Fieldstone: Rubble. Also, rough or unshaped stones used in construction, as in fireplaces.

Fillet: A flat, narrow, raised band coursing down a shaft of a column.

Finish: (A) elegance or refinement in a completed piece of work; especially in the workmanship or mechanical excellence of the work as distinguished from its design or significance. It is to be observed, however, that in some kinds of work the significance itself depends upon high or elaborate finish. Thus, in Florentine mosaic as applied to walls, or marble inlay as applied to pavements, the intended effect is not obtained without very perfect workmanship. (B) those parts of the fittings of a building which come after the heavy work of masonry, flooring, etc., has been done, and which are generally in plain sight and are closely connected with the final appearance of the building. The term is especially applied to interior work and often in connection with some other word forming a compound term.

Fireplace: A place where a fire can be built at the bottom of a chimney.

Flamboyant: (A) Having to do with the late French Gothic window traceries, which are so arranged that the openings between the stone piers are no longer circles, either with or without cusps, and triangles between the circles, but take the shapes of flames. The stone piers are cut in s curves and meet at acute angles, and the general aspect of the openings may be thought to resemble flames rising either vertically or at an angle with the vertical. The term is French, but in France the significance is generally applied to that which gives out flame or resembles flame, or to what is very brilliant and shining. It is less used in a strictly architectural sense in France than in England. (B) Having to do with the French Gothic of the late fifteenth and early sixteenth centuries; namely, that which has flamboyant window tracery. As this peculiar tracery prevailed in France from the close of the Hundred Years' War until about 1495, the term serves to describe the magnificent late Gothic, of which characteristic buildings are the church of S. Maclou at Rouen, the western part of the cathedral of Tours, the cathedral of S. Pol de Leon, S. Wulfran at Abbeville, the church of S. Riquier, not far from Abbeville, and the church of Brou at Bourg-en-Bresse.

Flashing: Pieces of sheet metal covering the joints or angles between a roof and any vertical surface against which it abuts, as of a wall, parapet, or chimney, to prevent the leakage or driving in of rain water; also, such pieces covering the hips and valleys of shingle or slate roofs, or the like; or covering the joints about window frames, etc., in frame buildings. Plain flashing is formed with a single strip turned up a few inches against the vertical surface to which it is tacked or otherwise secured, and running up under the slates, tiles, or shingles to a slightly higher level. For greater security an apron, usually of lead, may be affixed to the wall above the first strip, which it overlaps; the apron being driven into the joints of the masonry protects the joint of the flashing proper. Against a brick chimney or gable parapet the sloping joint is protected by step flashing; short pieces overlapping like slates replace the continuous strip, each turned into a different horizontal joint of the brickwork. Flashings against stonework are driven into grooves cut to receive them; in all cases the joint is cemented with common or elastic cement.

Fleche: A slender wood spire.

Flex: A metal channel that is flexible and used to convey electrical wiring.

Flexible Curve: A drawing device that can take the place of French Curves, and at the same time allow you to customize your own shapes. It also allows you to transfer a shape from one drawing to another.

Flight: An unbroken run of stairs.

Floor Plan: A sketch showing the doors, windows and interior design.

Floor Slab: A concrete floor that has been reinforced four inches thick.

Flooring: Materials used to lay a floor.

Flounce: A piece of fabric used to conceal the bottom of a chair.

Flue: The passage that carries the smoke up the chimney.

Flush: Even with, in the same plane with, something else, whether adjacent or not; in exact alinement with the surrounding surface. Thus, a flush panel has its surface in the same plane with the surrounding frame; two piers having the same projection from a wall may be said to have their outer faces flush. Within 1/4" maximum protrusion from surrounding surfaces.

Flushwork: Knapped flint used with dressed stone forming patterns of a tracery, etc.

Foil: A circular or nearly so shaped curve at the cusp of a circle or arch.

Footing Stone: Any stone intended for the construction of a footing; especially, a broad, flat stone for forming the base course of a foundation.

Footing: The lowermost part of a foundation wall, especially the wide base course, or the series of stepped courses which begin with stones or concrete three or four times as wide as the superstructure, and gradually grow narrower.

Force: The exertion of tension or motion.

Forms: Wood or metal molds that support a concrete mixture until it is set.

Formwork: Temporary metal or wood forms into which concrete is poured.

Forum: In Roman archaeology, a public market place or open square; used in earlier ages as the one principal center of a town. The Roman Forum (Forum Romanum; Forum Magnum) was the narrow valley between the Palatine Hill on the southwest, the Capitoline Hill on the northwest and the Viminal Hill on the northeast, the ground rising slowly toward the southeast to the Celian Hill. This small space could hardly be enlarged because of the rising ground on every side of it, and also because of the important buildings with which it was surrounded and which encroached upon it on every side. The temples whose ruins still remain were late edifices; but they stood on the sites of much earlier buildings, which sites were sacred and could not well be abandoned. But the building emperors seem to have been little inclined to enlarge the original forum even where that might have been done, on the northeast, but rather to have added open squares of their own which they surrounded with stately buildings and which vastly surpassed the Forum Magnum in splendor as well as in size. Besides those which are known to have existed, it is altogether probable that the great structures north of the Capitol, and which are associated with the names of the Antonine emperors, were also grouped around fora.

Fosse: A ditch used in defence.

Foyer: The entrance hall or entrance vestibule of a building.

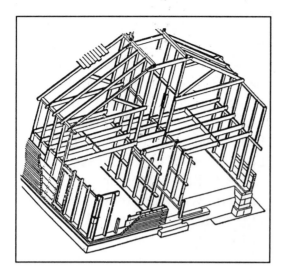

Frame House: In North America a wooden house.

Frame: (A) A structure of smaller parts brought together to form a whole; expecially, in building, an assemblage of slender and relatively long pieces (see framing). The carcase of a house, when of masonry, is not called the frame, but the skeleton of wood or ironwork put up for a building or part of a building is so designated. Frames may be composed of hollow parts, as tubes or boxes; thus, the common window frame of sliding sash windows is made of two upright boxes to contain the weights and cords, a sill below, and a head or yoke above. (B) A border prepared to enclose and isolate a picture, bas-relief, or the like. The use of the frame in strictly architectural practise is not very common, because the wainscoting, marble lining, stucco decoration, or the like, usually provides for the setting of whatever decorative panels may be inserted; but in some styles of decoration the frame is designed especially for the work of art, and in this case it may frequently be more or less movable. In Italy in the seventeenth century, paintings were often enclosed by extremely massive, carved, and coloured wooden frames, having 8 to 12 inches projection, and these often took varied forms, as oblong octagons, ovals, and the like. The picture, or other work of art, with its frame, would then be prepared for a definite place; but was capable of being used elsewhere. In like manner, the paintings of the Venetial school, applied to walls, and especially to the large flat ceilings of palaces and neoclassic churches, were framed with wood, carved and gilded, and the whole composition of many pictures and their frames has remained in place permanently for three centuries. Something of this is seen in the movable frames which are still retained as mounts for portraits and other paintings of the same period.

Framing, Baloon: In the United States, a system of framing wooden buildings in which the corner posts and studs are continuous in one piece from sill to roof plate, the intermediate joists being carried by girts spiked to, or let into, the studs, the pieces being secured only by nailing, without the use of mortises and tenons, or the like.

Framing: Originally and properly, the putting together of parts to produce a whole; the making of a structure of definite form and purpose out of parts especially prepared for it. In modern building, especially the putting together of slender and comparatively long pieces, such as beams, joists, girders, posts, and the like, of timber; or similar or corresponding parts of iron; or both in a skeleton; which skeleton is the essential structure of the building or part of the building. By a peculiar forcing of this signification, the term was formerly used by carpenters exclusively for the putting together of wood by means of mortises and tenons. This distinction disappears, of course, in ironwork of all kinds, and, in modern times, rarely obtains in any class of work.

Freestone: A stone that is easily cut in any direction, e.g.: sandstone or limestone.

French Curves: Plastic drafting tools used to draw curved segments of objects or plans. They are drawn against with pencil or pen after an appropriate segment is selected. A selection of two or three is usually enough for architectural drafting.

Frieze: A decorated strip along the upper section of a wall. The middle division of an entablature.

Frontispiece: The primary facade of a building.

Fulcrum: A support which allows free rotation about it.

Furnace: An apparatus by means of which a fire may be brought to a great heat, which heat may then be utilized in any way desired. Ordinarily, such a structure used for the heating of the interior of any building; in this sense, divisible into hot air furnace; although more commonly limited to the hot air furnace alone. Such a furnace is distinguished from a stove in that the hot air, collected in a large chamber, passes to different parts of the building by means of pipes and flues, whereas a stove generally heats the room in which it stands by direct radiation; although some part of the heat of the stove may be diverted, and the stove become, in a sense, a furnace.

Furring Strip: Any strip, generally of wood, used for furring. Specifically, in the United States, a strip of spruce, 1" x 2" in size, used chiefly in furring on the inner face of an outside wall to form an air space.

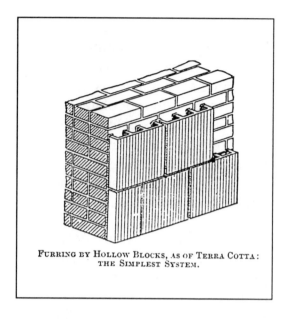

FURRING BY HOLLOW BLOCKS, AS OF TERRA COTTA: THE SIMPLEST SYSTEM.

Furring: A light framework, or simply strips, generally of wood, but sometimes of metal, applied to walls, beams, or similar surfaces to support sheathing, plaster, or other form of finish. Its purpose is either to give a more uniform and even structure for the application of such a finish; or to form an air space behind such a finish; or to give a semblance of a constructive form, as the imitation of a vault, by means of some plastic material carried on a frame of the necessary shape. By extension, in recent times, hollow brick or tile used for such purposes.

G

Gable End: In a building having a double pitch roof, one of the end walls which terminates at top in a gable.

Gable: A more or less triangular-shaped piece of wall closing the end of a double pitched or gable roof. The top of the wall may be bounded by the two slopes of the roof when this overhangs; or it may form a parapet following, more of less, the slopes of the roof behind. Hence, any piece of wall of the same general shape, having a more purely ornamental purpose. The French make a distinction between the *pignon*, which is properly the enclosure of the roof at either end, and the gable, which is more commonly ornamental; but in English no separate term has been introduced. It is often impossible to fix the lower boundary of a gable; but also very often a horizontal band, either of projecting moldings or of merely ornamental inlay, is carried across, usually for the artistic purpose of holding the parts firmly together in appearance. The only use of gables in classical architecture is in the pediments, and even this is rare in other than temple architecture. In the medieval styles, however, the gable, both constructive and ornamental, large and small, is a very important item in the general decorative system. In the earlier post-Gothic styles, especially in the north of Europe, such as the German Renaissance and the Elizabethan in England, the gable, whether forming a part of the main structure, or serving as the front of the dormer, is the chief decorative feature.

Galilee: A chapel or vestibule at the west end of a church.

Gallery: A mezzanine supported on columns overlooking the interior space of a building. The upper story above an aisle in a church. A large rectangular room used to display art. A shopping arcade. A railing that protects the exterior of furniture.

Galleting: Small pieces of stone inserted into mortar courses before it sets up.

Gargoyle: A carved grotesque figure which extends from a roof and serves as a water spout.

Gate: (A) A movable barrier, hung or sliding, which closes a gateway.

The distinction between door and gate is not observed; the term "gate" carries with it (1) the idea of closing an opening in a barrier, as a fence, wall, grating, or the like, rather than an opening into a covered building; (2) The idea of grating of iron or a framing of timber, rather than a solid and umpired valve or valves; but this distinction is not always observed, as when a large and important pair of doors are called gates, as city gates. Where there are solid doors closing a doorway into a public building, and outside of these are doors of iron grating meant to shut at night, the latter are often, and properly, called gates. (B) A gateway; hardly accurate in this sense, although common, especially in composition and in proper names.

Gazebo: A summerhouse in a park or garden. A look-out tower.

Geometrical Proportion: That theory of proportion in architecture which assumes the existence of a geometrical basis or system by which proportions may be determined and upon which the parts of the building may be put in the right place for producing the best effect.

Giant Order: See Colossal Order.

Girandole: A wall bracket, chandelier, or sconce carved elaborately usually found on a wall or projecting from a base.

Girder: Any, generally horizontal, member fulfilling the functions of a beam; differing from a beam only as being larger or of more complicated structure, or as being used for the support of other beams. In their more elaborate framed forms, girders are not to be distinguished from certain simpler forms of trusses. A beam of concrete, steel or timber used to support concentrated lead to various points.

Glass: A mixture of silica and some alkali resulting in a substance hard, usually brittle, a bad conductor of heat, and possessed of a singular luster. The most common kinds of glass are made by fusing together some ordinary form of silica, such as sand, with a sodium salt or some compound of potassium replacing the sodium either wholly or in part, and sometimes with lead. There is no formula of universal application; moreover, some varieties of glass contain ingredients which are kept secret by the maker, or are compounded in a way which is kept secret.

The different kinds of glass in use in architectural practice are: (1) clear glass in sheets more or less perfectly transparent and including ordinary window glass, plate glass, and several imitations of the latter, sometimes sold under the name of plate glass. Under this head come the various modern varieties of glass whose surface is deliberately roughened or ridged or furrowed or pressed in patterns with the purpose of reducing its transparency and allowing it to transmit light while shutting off the view of what may be beyond.

(2) Glass in small tesserae or in tiles of moderate size, usually opaque and very commonly colored. These are used for mosaic of the ordinary fashion, as in flooring and in the adornment of walls and vaults. The tiles are usually cast in one piece, in this resembling plate glass; and it is easy to produce very interesting bas reliefs and also inlaid patterns of great beauty, which may be complete in each tile or may require many tiles to complete the design. Such work was common among the Romans, who lined rooms with glass as freely as with marble. The tesserae, however, are more commonly cut from large

sheets by steel tools. The tesserae are sometimes gilded, and so prepared to give to a mosaic picture a background or partial decoration in gold, by making the glass tessera in two parts, laying a piece of gold leaf between the two, and uniting the whole by heat.

(3) Glass in sheets colored throughout its mass and used chiefly for decorative windows.

(4) Glass in sheets, flashed, as it is called; that is to say, colored by means of a finer coating of deep colored glass on one or on both sides. This device is used for colors which would be sombre if the whole substance were colored as in pot metal. The deep reds are the colors usually so treated. This also is used for decorative windows. Both the third and fourth kinds of glass are modified in many ways, especially in modern times, by the addition of an opaline tinge by the use of arsenic or other chemicals. The opalescent quality, when applied to otherwise uncolored glass, may be described as clouded with a whitish gray opacity, which, however, shows by transmitted light a ruddy spark. In the manufacture of glass for windows of great cost and splendor, it has been found that such

opalescent glass, when it has received strong and right color in addition to the opaline quality, is capable of more perfect harmony, tint with tint, or of a more harmonious contrast, color with color, than if the opaline character had not been given to it.

(5) Glass cast in solid prisms, and in prismatic and pyramidal shapes, for the purpose of being set in metal frames and used for vault lights.

(6) Glass in the body of which some foreign substance is introduced. This may be done with purely decorative effect, as by the artists of the Roman imperial epoch in vessels of considerable thickness and mass, and this has been imitated by the modern Venetian glassworkers. Wire glass is made on a similar plan for purposes of safety from fire.

(7) Soluble glass.

Golden Section: A classical proportion. It is defined as a line cut in such a way that the smaller section is to the greater as the greater is to the whole. It was considered a fundamental and divinely given design principal in the Renaissance.

Gopuran: A gateway in a South Indian temple.

Grain: (A) The fibers of wood taken together; the fibrous or strongly marked longitudinal texture of wood in which the sheaves of the sap vessels, all running one way, cause a marked distinction between the character of wood if cut crosswise or lengthwise of the log. Blocks for wood engraving are cut across the grain, but in nearly all other careful workmanship the end grain is avoided, and a perhaps excessive care is shown by modern carpenters and joiners never to allow this end grain (that is to say, the texture of the wood as shown when cut across) to be seen. Even in wood when cut in the direction of the grain, that is, lengthwise, there is a difference in the adhesiveness of the parts. Accordingly, as a log is cut into parts in the direction or nearly in the direction of the radii of one section of the log considered as a circle, the wood will be found tougher and less liable to split. It is well known that a log allowed to dry naturally will be found checked, or divided deeply by checks. If, then, parts are taken out of a log in such a way that the broad surfaces of these parts go in the direction of these checks, those parts will have little or no tendency to split. Advantage is taken of these circumstances to saw wood quartering, as it is called, the wood specially treated in this way being oak, on account of the open character of its grain. The term is used also to indicate the pattern or veining caused by the irregularity of the arrangement of the sap vessels and fibers. This, in some woods, is of great beauty, and it often happens that a knot, a part of the root, or even one of those curious warts or protuberances which are sometimes found projecting from the trunk of a large old tree, contains wood of a very beautiful pattern. The finest and most precious pieces of this kind are commonly sawed into thin veneers, which are then used by gluing them to thicker pieces of inferior wood. (B) To produce, by means of painting, an imitation, more or less close, of the natural grain of wood. The process is chiefly one of wiping, with a cloth held firmly upon the end of a stick, narrow bands in freshly laid paint; these bands showing light in contrast with the darker and thicker paint left on either side. If, for instance, paint of the color of walnut is laid over a lighter priming, a skilled grainer will use his wiping

tool with greater or less pressure, as he wishes to produce broader and paler or narrower and darker stripes. These stripes, kept close together and nearly parallel, constitute graining of the simplest kind. But the process in the more elaborate pattern is similar to this. (C) An embossed design impressed on a wallcovering. (D) The fibers in wood and their direction, size, arrangement, appearance or quality. When severed, the annual growth rings become quite pronounced and the effect is referred to as "grain."

(1) Flat Grain (F.G.) or Slash Grain (S.G.) lumber or veneer is a piece sawn or sliced approximately parallel to the annual growth rings so that some or all of the rings form an angle of less than 45 degrees with the surface of the piece. (2) Mixed Grain (M.G.) is any combination of Vertical or Flat Grain in the same member. (3) Vertical Grain (V.G.) lumber or veneer is a piece sawn or sliced at approximately right angles to the annual growth rings so that the rings form an angle of 45 degrees or more with the surface of the piece. (4) Quartered Grain is a method of sawing or slicing to bring out certain figures produced by the medullary or pith rays, which are especially

conspicuous in oak. The log is flitched in several different ways to allow the cutting of the veneer in a radial direction. (5) Rift or Comb Grain, lumber or veneer that is obtained by cutting at a angle of about 15 degrees off of the quartered position. Twenty-five percent (25%) of the exposed surface area of each piece of veneer may contain medullary ray flake. (E) The direction the fibers of a paper run as it is manufactured. It affects surface, directional patterns, folding, tear qualities and dimensional stability.

Grate: Originally and properly, a grating; in ordinary usage, that form of grating which is used to retain fuel in place while the air which supplies combustion passes freely upward from below between the bars. In this sense, especially, (1) a basket-like receptacle of bars as is used in an ordinary fireplace; sometimes hung by rings or sockets upon hooks built into the jambs, sometimes supported on feet, and in this latter case often called basket, or basket grate. Soft or bituminous coal is more commonly burned in grates of this last-named form. (2) The bottom, or floor, of a fire room or fire box in a furnace or stove of any sort. In this sense, usually and

normally flat and placed horizontally, but often arranged to revolve, to drop at one side while remaining supported on a pivot, or even to fold upon itself; these devices being for greater convenience in dumping the fuel when it is desired to clean the grate and start a fresh fire.

Grating: A structure of bars held together by cross pieces of any sort, or similar bars crossing one another in at least two directions, or, finally, of bars arranged in some more elaborate pattern. In this sense the term is equally applicable to a frame made of thick bars or beams of wood, and to a lighter and slender structure, as of metal. This is the generic term, and grate, grille, grillage are used in special senses. Gratings of wood are used to admit air and light, or to allow for vision through an obstacle, while at the same time ingress or egress is prohibited, or, when placed horizontally, an opening is made safe against persons or things falling into it accidentally. This is its most common use in building. The openwork partition across the parlor of a convent or the visitor's room in a prison is called by this name, although frequently the bars are wide apart and may even reach from floor to ceiling without cross pieces.

Groin: A sharp edge resulting from the intersection of vaulting surfaces.

Grotto: An artificial cave with waterfalls or fountains.

Ground Floor: Properly, that floor of a building which is most nearly on a level with the surrounding surface of the ground. By extension, same as Ground Story.

Ground Line (GL): The intersection of the ground plane and the picture plane. It is used as a measuring line.

Ground Plane (GP): This is the floor or ground of the scene. All vertical measures refer to this.

Ground Story: That story of a building the floor of which is nearly on a level with the surrounding surface of the ground. The term should be limited to such a story when its floor is not more than two or three steps above or below the sidewalk in a city, or the courtyard, greensward, or the like, nearest approaching it, in the country. Thus, in the case of a house with a high stoop, as in many American cities where the principal floor is seven

feet above the sidewalk, and the floor of the basement story is five feet below it, there is properly no ground story.

Ground: Anything used to fix a limit or to regulate the thickness or projection of the more permanent or of exterior finished work. The term is generally used in the plural; thus, grounds in ordinary building are pieces of wood secured to the jamb of a doorway, as in a brick wall, or to the base of a stud partition, to stop the plastering at the edge and to determine its thickness, and to these grounds the wooden trim may be nailed, or the grounds may be removed. Also, any strip secured to a wall, and more or less embedded in the plaster, to furnish a nailing, as to secure a wooden mantel, heady trim, or the like.

Grout: Concrete that is used as filler in between voids of joists. Mortar made thin for pouring into the interstices of a masonry wall; for spreading over a bed of concrete to form a smooth finish; and for other similar purposes where the use of stiff mortar is unpractical.

Gutter: A channel, trough, or like contrivance to receive and convey away water; whether in connection

with the roofs of a building, or
forming part of a pavement,
roadway, or the like. When used on
a building it may either form part of
a roof-covering turned up and
supported along, or near, the lower
edge of the slope; or it may be in the
form of a trough of metal or wood
hung from the edge of the roof; or it
may be part of a masonry structure
below, in which case perhaps of cut
stone and forming part of the cornice
or serving itself as the crowning
feature.

Gymnasium: A sport or gaming
building or place, from the Greek.

H

Half-timber: A wooden framework with another substance filling in the spaces.

Half-timbered: (A) Composed of timber so far as the framing is concerned, the spaces of which framing are then filled in with masonry in some form; this is the more usual meaning given to the term, but certain British authorities claim that such building as this is really whole timbered, the filling in by means of masonry having nothing to do with the construction in timber. (B) Having the lower story or stories of masonry, such as stonework, and the upper stories, or perhaps only the walls of the gables, framed of timber. This definition is given by those writers who object to the use of the term in the sense A. In building done in wood according to either definition, the timbers show on the outside, and are usually arranged so as to form a somewhat ornamental pattern. In this respect the buildings of some parts of the continent of Europe, such as Normandy and northwestern France in general, and large parts of Germany, are found more stately in design than the English examples; with more sculpture and a beautiful system of proportion. On the other hand, this system of building lasted long and was popular in England; the patterns of the framework itself were elaborate; and many valuable examples remain, even of stately country mansions, built in this way. It is a reasonable theory that during the reigns of James I and Charles I and the Restoration, country houses built by residents of London or nobles connected with the court were built of masonry according to the revived classical theories brought from Italy and France, while those built by proprietors who resided in the country were built according to the traditional methods with much use of timber. The filling of the spaces between the timbers was done sometimes with brickwork or rubble-stone masonry and sometimes by means of stout oak laths plastered on both sides. In case there were two sets of laths, one at the outer and one at the inner side of the wall, each set plastered on each side, there was obtained a very warm and solid filling.

Handrail: The railing along side a stair or steps used to maintain balance while climbing.

Hanger: A piece of metal used to support a suspended ceiling or a gutter. In the building trades, any contrivance, fixed or movable, for the suspension of any structure or member, usually, in combination.

Harmonic Proportions: An ancient system of architectural proportion built on musical harmony. The system is built on the fact that a plucked string one-half the length of an otherwise identical string will sound one octave higher. One fifth higher if the shorter is one two thirds and a fourth if the shorter is three quarters. Architects accordingly defined harmonious rooms or buildings as those which conformed to the same ratios. This system was rediscovered in the Renaissance and lauded, adopted and elaborated on by such theorists as Alberti and Palladio.

Hasp: A fastener for a door, lid, or the like, usually in the form of a plate or bar of metal hinged at one end, and with a slot or opening to receive a staple. A padlock, or in default of this a pin of wood or the like, being passed through the staple, the door, etc., is held fast.

Hatch: A rough door; the original signification being connected with the idea of grating or crib work, but in general use having equal application to that which is solid and uniform in surface; especially, (A) A heavy door filling the lower part of a doorway; either completed by a second heavy door above (see Dutch Door), or shut when the larger or more permanent door is opened, as when business of some kind is to be done across and above this lower door acting as a barrier or counter. (B) A door in a nearly horizontal position; in this sense like Trap, except that it conveys the idea of a much larger opening to be filled by the door in question. The hatches of ships are not hinged, but are lifted off and put on again so as to cover the Coaming, or in some cases are made to slide; but in architectural practice a hatch is usually hinged, and is often secured by a counterpoise, or is held in some way to avoid falling heavily when allowed to close. (C) By extension, the opening closed by a hatch. In this respect, exactly resembling the use of gate for gateway, door for doorway, and the like.

Hatching: Drawing by means of small and numerous lines laid close together. In freehand drawing, hatching may be used to produce effects of rounding and to distinguish shades from shadows, and the like. In architectural drawing, it is more commonly used to distinguish the cut or sectional parts from those shown in ordinary projection. Filling of an area in a drawing with a regular pattern of lines.

Haunch: The midway part of an arch and the point of greatest lateral thrust.

Header: Any piece or member which is laid in a direction transverse to a series of other similar members which abut against it. Specifically, (A) In the framing of a floor or roof, the piece which is framed into one or two trimmers, and which in turn supports the tail pieces. (B) In brickwork, and more rarely in building with cut stone, a piece of material, as a brick, having its length placed across the wall and serving to a certain extent as a bond.

Headroom: The clear space allowed above a flight of steps or a floor, platform, or the like, so that a person passing will have abundant room. The space should be sufficient to remove all sense of annoyance from the nearness of the floor or flight of stairs above. Thus, where stairs are

arranged, one flight above another, 7 feet in the clear vertically is the least space that should be allowed. As soon as a stair and its surroundings assume some architectural character, the headroom must be much greater than this, and its proper distribution is an important consideration in planning. By extension, the term is loosely applied to any space allowed vertically for a given purpose; as when an attic room is said to have 4 feet headroom at the low side nearest the eaves.

Hearth: A piece of floor prepared to receive a fire; whether in the middle of a room, as in primitive times, and in buildings of some pretensions-- the smoke being allowed to escape through openings in the roof; or, as in later times, the floor of a fireplace in the modern sense. The hearth of ancient times was sometimes raised above the floor, and then had often a low rim around it; and sometimes sunk beneath it, forming the bottom of a shallow pit. In either case it might be fitted with certain permanent holders for wood representing the dogs or andirons of later times. Some cooking hearths, as in Pompeii, are raised a foot or more above the floor, and are built of masonry, with an arched opening at one side in which fuel might have been kept. The hearth, then, includes properly the entire floor from the back lining of the fireplace to the outermost edge of the incombustible material. In builders' usage, however, it is very often customary not to include in the term the rougher flooring, as of hard brick, which is enclosed between the actual cheeks of the recess made in the wall or chimney breast. According to this custom, the hearth, or, as it might be called, the outer hearth, is usually a slab of slate, soapstone, marble or other fairly resistant material, which is placed outside of and beyond the fireplace proper. The mantelpiece in modern usage generally rests upon it, as do the fender and the front feet of the basket grate, or other fittings. A flooring of tile sometimes replaces the slab of stone. Whatever the material of the hearth, it is usually supported upon a flat arch of brickwork which often is built between the trimmers of the floor below. The area in front of the fireplace.

Heartwood: The wood formed at the interior or "heart" of a tree. It is quite free from sap,--the more so as the tree becomes older,--of finer and more compact and even grain, and therefore harder. It is usually considered better for general use than the outer portion of the trunk which contains the sap, and is, hence, known as sapwood. The latter has comparatively little strength and is more liable to rapid decay.

Herm: A rectangular pillar whose terminus has been carved into a head of Hermes or other figure. It was used as a boundary marker in Ancient Greece.

Hewn Stone: North American word for ashlar.

Hip: A sloping salient angle in a roof, where the slope of the roof changes direction, and one plane cuts or intersects another. Thus, in a double pitch roof where there are no gables, and where the ridge is shorter than either of the wall plates which run parallel to it, the roof falls back at a slope above the end walls, (which would otherwise be gable walls), and at either end two hips are formed.

Hod Elevator: A contrivance for raising a large number of loaded hods at one time. One of the forms is an endless chain resembling somewhat a flexible iron ladder; this serves for the workmen to use in ascending, or, when set in motion, for carrying up the hods.

Hod: A box for carrying building materials, especially mortar; usually shaped like a trough and with a pole secured to the bottom. The trough or box being set upon the laborer's shoulder, the pole serves to steady and balance the load. Hods are now usually raised to the scaffolding by machinery of some kind.

Hoist: An appliance for raising passengers or materials to a height, as to a scaffold or within a building to an upper floor. In its simplest form it was merely a tackle operated by a horse or by hand. In its more elaborate forms, as when operated by steam, electricity, etc., it is not to be distinguished from an elevator except, possibly, as being rougher or having simpler machinery or lower speed. The two terms are often used as synonymous.

Hoistway: The vertical passage or channel through which a hoist of any kind ascends. Thus, in buildings, it is commonly provided that the hoistway, or the clear space carried through the floors from top to bottom, shall be enclosed with

solid partition or with gratings to prevent accidents.

Holdfast: An implement for securing anything in place, or which when secured itself to a solid structure makes easy the fixing of other more movable parts to it.

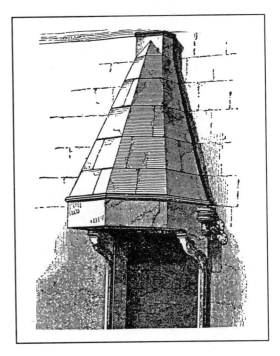

Hood: A rooflike canopy over an opening, especially over a fireplace. In particular:--(A) In medieval and later architecture, a structure of masonry or of plaster work held by a frame of wood or the like, which is entirely secured and protected by the plaster, and projecting from a wall above a hearth. The flue for the smoke passes upward from the tope of the hood, and is generally concealed in the wall. Such hoods are sometimes carried on projecting cheek pieces or jamb pieces, so that the fireplace is partly enclosed on three sides. They were also sometimes carried on long corbels projecting from the wall, or on light columns, one or more on either side. (B) In modern usage, a light pyramidal or conical covering as of iron suspended over the furnace of a laboratory or the like, or even a cooking range, either hung free from the ceiling or supported on light uprights or set against the wall, as the furnace, etc., stands free or has one side engaged. The use of such a hood is mainly for ventilation; sometimes very important to prevent disagreeable or noxious smells from pervading the building. A flue and special provision for the circulation of air in the flue are therefore necessary.

Horizon Line: The line that runs parallel to the ground line and intersects the center or the view on the picture plane. This corresponds to the eye-level of the observer. In interior perspective it is usually five or five and one-half feet above the ground line.

Hornwork: A military outwork made up of two demi-bastions connected by a curtain and joined to the main work by two parallel wings.

Housing: (A) A groove, recess, or the like, cut or formed in one piece, usually of wood, for the insertion of the edge or end of another. (B) Any light, houselike structure, as for a temporary shelter.

Hung: Secured in place as described under Hanger and Hanging; especially, secured in such a way that the object so secured is free to move within certain limits; thus, a door or shutter is hung when it is secured by its hinges to the jamb or doorpost, and the sliding sash of a window is hung by means of cords which pass through a pulley and are secured to weights.

Hypocaust: The underground chamber of Roman central hot air heating systems.

Hypogeum: An underground room.

Hypostyle: A large space covered by a roof supported on rows of columns.

Hypotrachelium: The groove
between the shaft and the necking
on a Doric column.

I

Iconostasis: In the Greek church a screen between the sanctuary and the body of the church; usually in one plane only; a wall built from side to side of a sanctuary and having three doorways. The term signifies *image bearing*, derived evidently from the habit of covering the screen with paintings. It appears to be a general rule in the Greek Church to conceal from the laity the altar itself and the celebration of the mass. In a Coptic church a screen conceals the three altars, as in the Greek church it conceals the single altar. The term in Egypt is Haikal Screen or sanctuary screen. There are seventh century examples of which the icons are of ivory inlaid in the woodwork. The doorways mentioned above are commonly filled by curtains which are dropped at the time of the celebration of the mass. In ancient times these seem to have been uniformly filled with solid doors, as is still the case among the Coptic churches. There are, however, more variations of the type, both ancient and modern, than is generally assumed. Thus, in some existing churches, there is an outer and an inner solid screen, the inner one opening into the sanctuary proper but still having three doors in all the well-known instances. Whether the name inconostasis is equally applied in ritual usage to both the outer and the inner screen does not appear. The essential characteristics of this Eastern form of chancel screen are, then, its height, its solidity, its being covered with paintings, or in the most ancient examples, with inlays, and its being employed to shut off entirely from the congregation the view of what is going on within the sanctuary.

If of large size, the metal sash bars are shaped with gutters to carry off the water of condensation, and glazed with sheets of fluted or rough plate glass, varying from 12" x 48" and 3/16" thick to 20" x 100" and 6/16" thick. If ordinary double thick glass is used, the sheets are from 9" to 15" wide, and from 16" to 30" long. In metal sash bars or mountings these sheets are set without putty. Skylights are often provided with ventilators arranged to be opened or closed by cords from below, and a flat decorated inner skylight is frequently placed beneath the outer skylight in a ceiling panel, when it is desired to make this feature an element in an architectural composition as seen from beneath. Sometimes, as in the covering of interior courts, winter gardens, exposition buildings, conservatories, marquises or canopies, and horticultural buildings, the entire roof is a skylight, and is emphasized as an especial architectural feature, the frame in such cases being of iron or wood. Occasionally smaller skylights are in the form of glazed scuttles arranged to be opened for access to the roof.

Imbrex: A convex tile covering the joint between the flat or concave roofing tiles. Used in Roman and Greek architecture.

Impost Block: A splayed sided block occurring between the abacus and capital on a column.

Impost: A wall member contained in a wall and seemingly supporting the end of an arch.

Impulvium: Rectangular basins in the center of the atrium of a Roman house.

Inclination: Slope of any kind; especially in building that has to do with decorative effect as contrasted with Batter, which is the slope of walls made thicker at the base for strength, or in a fortification for defence; and slope which is more commonly applied to a roof or ramp of a staircase. Thus, the axes of a Doric column in Greek work are found to have been generally inclined to the vertical, and in medieval work, walls and pillars are continually set with an incline. The angle of inclination is that which a roof, a ramp, or other essentially sloping member makes, either with the horizon, that is to say, with the horizontal plane, or with a vertical plane. It is rare that this is estimated by builders in terms of mathematical science, as in so many degrees and minutes. More commonly it is estimated by the horizontal dimensions compared with the vertical dimensions. Thus a carpenter will say that the inclination of his roof is three (horizontal) to two (vertical).

Incrustation: The covering of any thing with an outer shell or "crust." (A) The covering of a whole surface with such a material, as when a wall of brick is entirely concealed with marble slabs or with mosaic. (B) The adornment or diversifying of a surface by partial covering which is, however, of considerable proportionate size. Thus, a brick wall may be adorned with incrustations of marble covering a fourth or a sixth of its whole surface, and the term would not be used for the mere inlaying of a few narrow bands. A metal box is said to have incrustations of enamel, or to be adorned with incrusted enamels, when the enamels themselves are somewhat elaborate compositions and are affixed as entire works of art upon the surface.

Indent: A stone niche carved to hold a statue or object.

Indentation: The diversifying of a surface, an arris, a Molding, or the like, by depressions or hollows; usually in a series. Ornamentation by this means is usually confined to early and barbarous work, but the beautiful Venetian moldings are practically a series of indentations, and the edge of a slab of marble, or a board, as the shelf of a bookcase, or the like, is often ornamental by one or more series of notches which may be varied in size, in order, or in place.

Inglenook: A recessed area next to a fireplace for a seat.

Inlaid Work: Decoration by inserting a piece of one material within an incision or depression made for it in another piece of material. The term is usually confined to a combination in this way of hard materials; as black marble in white, or, as in some marble pavements in Florentine mosiac, etc., of many different colored materials on a plain background; but it is extended to mean incised work filled with paste which becomes hard after a little while. Inlays in wood, if Italian in their design or their origin, are called *Tarsia* or *intarsiatura*. Surfaces made up of many small parts fitted together are properly mosaic, no matter how large the pieces are, because in this case, as in the fine mosaics of a vault, there is no continuous and solid background in which the other pieces are inlaid. A patch of mosaic may, however, be inlaid upon a larger surface.

Intercolumniation: (A) The space between the shafts of two adjacent columns. (B) The ratio of the diameter of a shaft to the space between two shafts. An intercolumniation is usually considered the distance in the clear between the lower parts of the shafts; sometimes, however, it is taken as the distance from center to center of columns. Ordinarily, it is described in terms of the diameter or semidiameter taken at the bottom of the shaft, though its absolute dimension may of course be used. The term, though not necessarily limited to classic styles, is chiefly employed in describing classic colonnades. The terminology of the subject is derived from Vitruvius, who describes five kinds of temples, as follows: Picnostyle, with columns set 1 1/2 diameters apart; systyle, 2 diameters; eustyle, 2 1/4, with a central intercolumniation of 3 diameters; diastyle, 3 diameters, of which he says the architraves often fail through being too long; and finally, araeostyle, a window spacing with architraves of wood.

Interlace: To cross and recross, as if woven; said of different cords, bands, withes, or the like, or of a single piece of flexible material returning upon itself. By extension, to seem to interlace, as of a sculptured ornament resembling a band crossing and recrossing itself, or of several bands seeming to cross one another, first above, then below.

Intrados: The inner curve of an arch. A soffit.

Ionic Order: One of the five orders recognized by the Italian writers of the sixteenth century. The order is of Greek origin, although it received a greater development on the shores of Asia Minor, a country inhabited by the Ionian Greeks, than in the mother land itself; yet the earliest existing buildings which are assuredly of this style are of the main land of Greece, and other great islands which have always been closely connected with it. This remark applies only to the fully or partially developed Ionic order, for what are called proto-Ionic capitals have been found in considerable numbers in the non-Greek lands farther removed from the shores of the Mediterranean as well as in Greece itself.

The most important instances of the, as yet, imperfect Ionic capital are still, however, those found at Athens, in some ruins on the Trojan plain, thought to be those of the ancient Neandria, at Naucrates in Egypt, and in the islands of Delos and Lesbos. In all of these the capital is almost devoid of horizontal lines, and consists of two volutes which spring from the shaft, as if the designer had studied a reed or other succulent stem of circular section which had been split for a short distance down the middle and rolled away from the center in two scrolls. In some cases, this appearance of nature study is made stronger by the introduction into the design of a strongly marked and sometimes double band which surrounds the circular shaft just above the separation of the two volutes. In others, as in a well known example at Athens, covered with brilliant painting, the capital has gone a step farther in its development, and is a solid block adorned merely by the appearance of two scrolls treated from the same common center. All these proto-Ionic capitals tend to overset the theory advanced by some archaeologists, reasoning backward from the developed capital, that the decoration by volutes came of the adornment of a horizontal block, the ends of which were carved in this easy and obvious way. The perfected capital is, indeed, not wanting in strongly marked horizontal lines, and even those of earlier times than that of the highest development, as perhaps of the sixth century B.C., like one recently discovered at Delphi, show a very strongly marked flat table, the ends of which only are worked into the volutes. This flat table being supported by an ovolo Molding,

forming a complete circle and resting upon the shaft, and adorned with very large oves, needs nothing but the refinement of its parts to make it the perfected capital of the Erechtheum. This refinement was more needed in the Ionic capital than in some others, because the form is in itself somewhat irrational, and suggests in a disagreeable way the oozing out of a more plastic material under the superincumbent weight. Thoughts of this kind disappear when the highly wrought design of the fifth century capital is studied. The fluting of the shaft does not appear in the earliest examples; but, in those which seem to be of the fifth century, like that of Delphi mentioned above, there are channels like those of the Doric columns, but more numerous, and in the fifth century these are succeeded by the well known flutings, twenty-four in number, and separated by narrow fillets instead of meeting at the sharp arises, as in the channels named above.

The base underwent fewer important changes during the period of which we can judge, for the practice of fluting horizontally the large torus of the base came in at a very early epoch, and this remained the most important characteristic of the order after the volutes of its capital. When the Ionic shaft is set upon the Attic base, it loses much of it distinction. The bases of the little temple of Nike Apteros at Athens seem to combine the two ideas, the combination of flutes resting upon a part, at least, of the Attic base; and a somewhat similar attempt was made in the famous Erechtheum. The flutings and the arrangement of the base are of peculiar importance to students, because the Corinthian order when it began was, in the main, the Ionic order with a newly invented capital. In connection with the Ionic order there are some beautifully imagined ornamental devices in less common use. Thus, the pilasters which are used with the Ionic column are sometimes of singular beauty, having simply fluted shafts with a capital consisting of a band of anthemions, with egg and dart moldings above, and a base with rich flutings and sometimes a kind of guilloche adorning the torus. Moreover, it is in connection with this order that the most perfect instance of the caryatid occurs, namely, in the Erechtheum at Athens. The entablature and the other parts of the temple seem to have been the subject of thought and study as careful as that given to buildings of the Grecian Doric order.

The frieze, having no triglyphs, is sometimes adorned with a continuous band of figures, those of the Erechtheum having been planted on and made of different material, so as to show some contrast of color, even without the use of painting and gilding. The frieze of the temple of Nike Apteros, above alluded to, was also adorned with figures on a very small scale. Ionic temples were numerous on the Grecian shores of Asia Minor and Syria. The most curious instance of the introduction of the order in a place which seems incongruous is the well known portico of the Propylaea of the Acropolis at Athens. There, while the outer colonnades on both sides are pure Doric of a perfect type, the columns which front upon the continuous passage of the roadway through the portico from west to east are Ionic; but of necessity their entablature is very far removed from the full perfection of the order.

Iron, Cast: Iron which is shaped by being run into a Mold while melted, as described under casting. In ordinary commercial usage a compound of iron and carbon; the material which runs directly in liquid form from the blast furnace, and which hardens in the Mold. From cast iron is made the purer iron which is used for working with the hammer, and also steel. Cast iron is brittle and hard, and is not capable of being welded, that is to say, of having two parts united when hammered together while hot,--the property in iron which is most important to it as a material for decoration.

Iron, Channel: An iron or steel member shaped as a channel; especially one having the form of a small channel beam, which see under Beam.

Iron, Galvanized: Iron coated with zinc. The purpose of so protecting iron is to prevent rusting by keeping the moisture from its surface. It is, however, common to paint thoroughly all articles of galvanized iron as soon as they are put into place. (A) Properly, iron which has been covered first with tin by galvanic action, and subsequently with zinc by immersion in a bath. (B) In common usage, but improperly, iron which has been so coated by a non-galvanic process; having been immersed hot in a bath of zinc and other chemicals which form an alloy on the surface of the iron. (C) A hard iron that softens when heated enough to be molded into desired shape. It contains less than .02 percent of carbon. This is of peculiar importance, beyond that of any other hammered metal work, because partly of the abundance and the hardness of iron, but more especially on account of its power of being welded and forged. The whole system of ornamental wrought-iron work, by which the buildings of the Middle Ages of the Renaissance were beautiful throughout Europe, depends upon this property, possessed by iron alone among metals, of adhering firmly one part to another when these are first heated to a certain temperature and are then hammered together. Thus when a hinge of wrought iron is to be made for a church door with deliberate decorative purpose, it is easy to terminate each strap by a series of branches, partly by cutting the strap iron itself and bending one sprig or branch away from the others, and partly for forging other slender bars and the like, which can be welded to the original stem. The difficulty with such iron work is, however, its extreme liability to rust and the consequent necessity of doing something to protect the surface. It is in this connection that gilding has become so common in the case of ironwork. Magnificent grilles of the eighteenth century and other modern imitations of equal refinement and elaboration, if of less original beauty, are commonly gilded in great part, and this extensive gilding often injures greatly their general effect.

Iron: (A) A metal which in practical use is approximately pure only in the form known as wrought iron. This is peculiarly malleable and has the remarkable quality of being susceptible of welding, that is, of uniting one piece to another, when both are heated to a certain high temperature and are then hammered together. Cast iron contains much carbon; this, in the form in which the melted metal flows from the melting furnace, is called pig iron, the term cast iron being reserved for that which has been remelted and cast in molds for special purposes. As compared with wrought iron, this is brittle and not malleable, and it is not susceptible of being welded. Until recently, ironwork in architecture was limited to these two forms of the metal; cast iron was found to have a great resistance to superincumbent weight, and made admirable columns, especially when cast in thin shells, cylindrical or prismatic in outward section, and having a comparatively large hollow core. Wrought iron, on the other hand, was singularly tough, tenacious, and capable of bearing a very great tensile strain; it was, therefore, fit for ties of all forms. It was also perfectly well adapted to support vertical pressure, and at a time when the American cities were being filled with facades of cast iron, similar structures on the continent of Europe were being made of wrought iron almost exclusively, the uprights being formed of plates bolted together much on the principle of hollow build beams. Steel, which has less carbon than cast iron, is to a certain degree malleable and capable of being welded; its peculiar value is, however, in its capacity for being tempered by means of which a very high degree of hardness can be reached. By modern processes of manufacture, steel has been made easy and cheap of production, and its use for rolled beams, built beams, build columns, and the like, is superseding the use of wrought iron and of cast iron. (B) Any small or subordinate member of cast or wrought iron.

Iwan: A vaulted hall open at one or both ends. Occurs in Islamic architecture.

J

Jack: In building, an apparatus for raising, lowering, or sustaining a part of a building; consisting, in its usual and simplest form, of a vertical screw which is raised or lowered when turned in a fixed nut, and the top of which supports the given load.

Jamb Shaft: A shaft with capital and base fastened to the jamb of a door or window.

Jamb: One of the lateral upright surfaces of an opening; hence, also, a piece forming, or intended to form, the side of an opening. In thick walls, the door jamb is often richly panelled; in the Middle Ages, the jambs of doorways in very heavy walls were commonly splayed with a stepped section and enriched with moldings and jamb shafts. The side of a door frame, doorway, or window; usually the side on which the opening for the lock is placed.

Jetty: The projecting upper story of a timber-framed house.

Jib: A concealed flush door painted or decorated to match the wall into which it is cut.

Jigsaw: A saw that has a long small blade used in cutting fretwork or latticework.

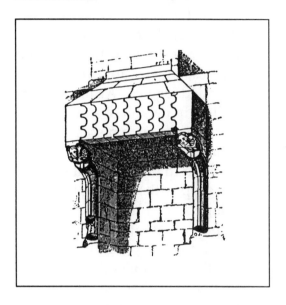

Joggle: A projection, as a tongue or shoulder, formed on a piece, or member, which it serves to unite to another adjoining, either by the insertion of the joggle into a corresponding notch or recess, or by its overlapping a similar projection on the adjoining piece. Hence, a separate piece, as a dowel of key, used for the same purpose by its insertion into the aperture framed by two adjoining recesses. In the latter connection the term is more commonly restricted to masonry. The term is not very definite, and is extended to include various methods of such joining and decorative and structural projections for which there are no more specific terms. Thus, the stiles of a window sash may extend below the rail, to afford greater support for the tenons of the latter, these downward projections being called joggles. Again, the term is applied, in default of a more accurate one, to such pieces of stonecutting as enable stones to hold one another in place, so that one cannot drop without being broken or breaking its neighbors. Thus, the lower part of Smeaton's lighthouse tower, on the Eddystone rock, was built entirely of stones dovetailed together and further secured by joggles, and in like manner the elaborate polychromatic masonry of some medieval, and many Islamic, buildings has many curved archivolts and flat arches used to replace lintels which are composed of stones cut with joggles.

Joinery: Joiners' work; the interior fittings of dwellings, etc., dadoes, door trim, and the like. The term would be more appropriate for the entire decorative woodwork of interiors than for cabinet work, but has nearly become obsolete, at least in the United States.

Joint, Expansion: A joint that allows something to expand or contract.

Joint: (A) Any beam intended primarily for the construction or support of a floor, ceiling, or the like, and horizontal or nearly so. By extension, a sleeper as used for the support of a wooden floor over a masonry or fireproof floor. (B) Locally, in the United States, a stud or piece of scantling about 3" x 4" in size. Split Joint. A piece of scantling as defined under Joint, B, but of half the size. (B) The place at which two parts, or pieces, meet, and sometimes unite; the surfaces so brought together considered collectively; also the space between two such faces, which may or may not be filled with a cohesive material to unite the two parts; hence, the mass of cohesive material so placed. Any two pieces brought into more or less close contact form a joint between them. A wall built of stones without the use of mortar is said to have dry joints (see bed). Again, it may be required that brickwork is to be laid in certain mortar with 3/8' joints, such stipulation referring to the thickest of the mass of mortar between the bricks. Again, two timbers may be framed by a mortise and tenon joint, the term in such case being applied to the several contiguous surfaces, together with the parts immediately connected. In connecting lead pipes end to end, the solder forms a homogeneous mass completely enveloping the butting ends, the whole assemblage being known as a wiped joint. Joints having specific compounded names derived from their formation or mode of connection (as, e.g., dovetail joint) are not defined here, as their meaning is self-evident from the use of the attributive term.

Joists, Exposed: Joists whose undersides are exposed to the room below. They are often molded to trim.

Joists: Parallel horizontal timbers laid between walls or beams to carry floorboards.

K

Keep: A castle's primary tower. Used as a living-quarter.

Keeper: A metal plate set in a door jamb for a door bolt.

Key: (A) An instrument for fastening and unfastening a lock; capable of being inserted or withdrawn at pleasure, and when withdrawn, leaving the lock incapable of being opened or shut except by violence. The principal parts of an ordinary key are as follows: Bow--the enlargement at one end of the shank whereby the key is turned by the fingers. Bit--the lug at the end of the shank which fits into the lock and raises the tumbler and turns the bolt of the lock. The bit is cut and grooved to fit itself to the various wards and levers of the lock. Shank--the shaft connecting the bow and bit. In the East, keys are commonly of wood, and a series of metal pins set into the wooden bar of the key can be adjusted to holes on the lock, thus raising tumblers and allowing the latch to be withdrawn. The metal keys of the Middle Ages and the succeeding centuries were often the medium of exquisite decoration, not merely in the graceful and picturesque proportion of the parts of the key proper,--bit, shank, and bow; but also in the way of delicate chasing and even elaborate inlay of other materials than iron. Locks and keys of extraordinary beauty have been preserved when the wooden chests which they were made for have disappeared, and these are among the jewels of our collections of ornamental art. (B) A wedge, or a tapering piece or member, used singly, or in pairs, as a means of drawing two parts together and tightly securing them when it is forced into an aperture prepared for the purpose; or as a means of holding two members or surfaces apart; hence, a member for a similar purpose, whether so shaped or not, designed for insertion into recessed in two or more adjoining parts, and commonly secured in place by wedges or keys of the specified form. Thus a key may be used instead of a cleat for securing together a number of boards edge to edge; and will be itself formed of a tapering board forced into a corresponding groove cut across the assembled boards; the cross section of such a key and its corresponding groove has usually a dovetail shape, flaring inward, for greater security. A common use of keys is in heavy framing, as in forming a scarf joint, or assembling the parts of a truss. For the last purpose, a key is commonly of iron, and known as a cotter, and used in connection with a gib, or gibs. (C) In plastering, or similar work, that part of the plastic material which enters into the interstices, or clings to the rough surface, of the backing or prepared support; and by its adherence sustains the coat of mortar, or like material. Thus, the first coat of plaster applied to lathing forms a key when pressed through the spaces arranged for it; and this coat being "scratched" or roughened enables the next coat to form a key.

Keystone: The central stone of an arch or rib vault

Kiln Dried: Lumber dried in a closed chamber in which the removal of moisture is controlled by artificial heat and usually by controlled relative humidity.

Kiln: A heated room used to dry lumber or an oven used to fire ceramics.

King-post: A vertical timber standing centrally on a tie-beam and

rising to the apex of the roof where it supports a ridge.

Kiosk: A small open pavillion. A small shop in a park or on a street side. A polygonal or cylindrical sign board or information booth.

Knapped Flint: Flint split into two pieces and laid so that the smooth black surfaces of the split sides form a wall.

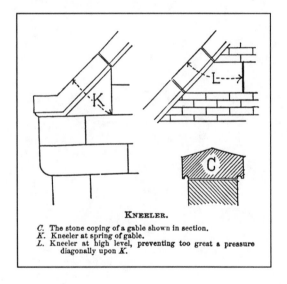

KNEELER.

C. The stone coping of a gable shown in section.
K. Kneeler at spring of gable.
L. Kneeler at high level, preventing too great a pressure diagonally upon K.

Kneeler: A stone block set at the top of a masonry wall to finish the eaves or coping. A piece of church furniture padded and used to kneel on during prayer.

Knob: A rounded projection; in architecture sometimes a piece of

utility, as when furnishing the
handle to a door lock, or door latch,
and sometimes an ornament.   In
this latter sense the term implied
generally the termination of a
slender and isolated member.

L

Labyrinth: (A) In Greek archaeology, a complicated building, with many corridors and rooms, through which it was difficult to find one's way. The term also is applied to a cave. The Labyrinth of Egypt is described by Herodotus and Strabo, but the ruins as they exist near the ancient Lake Moeris, in the province of Fayoum, show no trace of the splendor of the buildings as they describe them. The Labyrinth of Crete, in which Minotaur was confined, is perhaps wholly mythical. The Labyrinth in the tomb of Porsena at Clusium was apparently merely the tomb itself but a building so large and of such unusual character for a tomb that the term was applied to it in admiration. (B) A maze of any description. In modern times, generally a fantastic arrangement of lofty and thick hedges in a garden, as at Hampton Court, where it is somewhat difficult to find one's way to the center. (C) A drawing or other representation on a flat surface of a maze, so elaborate that, even with the whole plan before him, the student is puzzled as to the right course to follow to reach the center. In architecture such labyrinths are inlaid in the pavements of churches of the Middle Ages, where they are sometimes thirty feet or more in diameter. They were supposed to be emblematic either of the difficulty and uncertainty of the Christian's progress through this world, or they were, as some think, of purely mystical meaning, connected with some legend now lost and held traditionally by the masons. It has been remarked that they contain no religious emblems whatever. They were very numerous in the Middle Ages, but a great number of them were destroyed when the pavements were relaid.

Laced Windows: Windows visually connected by colored bricks.

Lacquer: Properly, a substance made of lac, that is to say, of the substance sold as gum-lac, stick-lac, seed-lac, shell-lac or shellac; but by extension applied also to a varnish made in Oriental countries from the sap of certain plants. Persian, Indian, and Chinese lacquers are hardly of importance in architecture. Japanese lacquer is chiefly made from the tree Rhus Vernicifera. Lacquer ware made with this material is well known in the shops, the finest pieces being of very great value to collectors and to students of Oriental art; so that a box a few inches in length may bring several hundred dollars in public auction. Such lacquer is applied to the decoration of temples and other public buildings in Japan much as paint is used among European nations, but the perfect surface, permanent glass and delicate color of the lacquer gives it a peculiar charm.

Lacunar: A coffered or panelled ceiling.

Lady Chapel: A chapel dedicated to the Virgin Mary.

Lanai: A Hawaiian term for a verandah or terrace that has been covered.

Lancet Window: A thin pointed window in the form of an arch.

Landing: (A) That portion of a floor, or a confined floor space, immediately adjoining or connected with a staircase or flight of stairs; it may be either the floor space meeting the foot or top of a flight. (B) Any structure, or part of a structure, at the water's edge, at which persons or goods can be embarked or disembarked. In this sense often landing place.

Landscape architecture: The design of a garden using flowers, trees, shrubs and borders to achieve a balanced effect of colors.

Lantern Cross: A churchyard cross topped in the shape of a lantern.

Lantern: In architecture:--(A) Any structure rising above the roof of a building and having openings in its sides by which the interior of the building is lighted. By extension, such as architectural feature whether serving as a means of lighting the interior or not. The tower built over the crossing of a cruciform church is often so called, especially when open, and light rather than massive, as that above the octagon at Ely cathedral (of wood), and that of S. Ouen at Rouen, though of stone and very large. The uppermost large member of a cupola is so called: that of Florence cathedral is very large and heavy, about 80 feet high above the curve of the cupola. (B) A structure for surrounding and protecting a beacon or signal light, as on a lighthouse, having sides of glass held by the slightest framework practicable. (C) An eighteenth century oil lamp with a candle in the lamp or lantern or a modern light fixture suspended from the ceiling or a wall.

Latch, Night: One intended primarily for use at night; usually, a form of Latch Lock

Latch, Thumb: A latch as described in the general definition above; the outer end of the lever terminating in a flat or concave plate so adjusted that the thumb presses upon it easily while the fingers grasp an independent curved handle below.

Latch: Originally and properly, a form of door bar which is permanently secured to the door by a pivot at one end, the other end being free to fall into a slot or hook, out of which it must be raised to allow the door to open. There is also, generally, a projecting member near the edge of the door beneath the bar which is thus prevented from falling when the door is open. In its primitive form such a latch was raised from the outside by a string passing through a hole in the door, which string was drawn in when security was desired; and later by a short lever passing through the door beneath the bar and working on a pivot. This is essentially the construction of the modern so-called

thumb latch. In modern times, the meaning of the term is extended to include spring locks designed especially for outer doors.

Lath, Counter: (A) An intermediate lath or batten interposed between a pair of Gauge Laths. (B) One of a supplementary set; as when laths are nailed across others used as furring.

Lath, Gauge: In roofing, one of a number of laths placed by accurate measurement so as to support a tile or slate at the proper points, as at the nail holes.

Lath, Metallic: A preparation of metal, usually wrought, rolled, or drawn iron, to receive plastering by having openings which give a good key or hold to the plaster, and which is also capable of being secured to woodwork or metal work in the construction. The most common form has heretofore been a coarse wire netting with the mesh of 3/4" or thereabout, and this is commonly called wire lath. Many more recent types are in the market, generally consisting of thin plates of metal in which openings are cut, the strips which are cut from the openings being left attached by one or two edges and forced into a different plane. Good three-coat plaster upon a solid and well-secured surface of metallic lath has been found to have exceptionally good powers of resistance to fire. Also called wire lath.

Lath: A strip of metal or wood, generally quite thin and narrow, but often approaching a batten or furring strip in size; a number of which are intended to be secured to beams, studs, and such members for the support of tiles, slates, plaster, and similar finishing materials.

Lattice: A system of small, light bars crossing each other at regular intervals. In modern country houses this is often made of laths, or light slips of wood forming regular square or lozenge-shaped openings. In Oriental work, as in the houses of Cairo and other Middle Eastern cities, the projecting windows are filled with very elaborate lattices. A similar filling for windows was once common in England, replacing glass, and shutting out much of the snow and rain. A lattice painted red was the sign of the tavern. The term is extended to cover glazed sash in which the sash bars form square or lozenge-shaped openings filled with pieces of glass of the same shape. Also, in recent times and in composition, a large structure of

similar form. Thus, an iron girder having a web composed of diagonal braces is commonly known as a lattice girder. A distinction is sometimes made in iron construction, between latticing and lacing: the former applying to a double diagonal system or bars crossing each other; the latter restricted to mean a single series arranged in zig-zag.

Lavabo: (French) Table and washstand. An eighteenth century wash basin found below a wall fountain.

Lead holder: The lead holder with loose lead is superior to wood-clad pencils for drafting. It can hold any hardness of lead, and can quickly be changed and sharpened with the lead pointer. "F" lead is standard for all-around drafting.

Leaded Lights: Rectangular or diamond-shaped leaded panes which form a window.

Leroy Lettering Set: A plastic template used to guide a scriber with an ink pen to letter many sizes and styles of type on plans and drawings. This is an excellent way for neat titles. Sets come with as few as three lettering templates and a scribe.

Lesbian Cymatium: Cyma Reversa Molding enhanced with leaf and dart.

Leveller: Anything intended to bring about a level--i.e. a horizontal surface; any contrivance by which the upper surface of a structure may be brought to a horizontal or nearly horizontal plane. Especially in stone masonry, a stone of the proper dimension to make up a difference in height between two adjoining stones, so as to produce a level bed for the next course above; also a flat stone for making a level bearing, as in a footing course.

Light: In architecture, (A) The volume of daylight received in a room, corridor, or the like. The term is often used in composition, as in the subtitle Borrowed Light. By extension, a similar volume of light from an artificial source; as a closet may have a borrowed light from a room lighted by electricity. (B) An opening or medium through which daylight may pass, as a pane (called generally by glaziers and carpenters a light) of glass. More especially the opening between two mullions or window bars in a decorative window, the glass of which is commonly in irregular or other small pieces, hardly called lights in this case. (C) An artificial source of light; a means of providing light, as in the compound or qualified terms gas light, electric light. Thus, in arranging for the lighting of an interior, it may be stipulated that ten lights be ranged along the cornice on either side. (D) The manner or the nature of the illumination received by a picture or other work of art, or by a wall or ceiling considered as the medium for the display of such works of art. Thus, it may be said that there is no good light for pictures on the east wall. (E) Radiant energy that is capable of exciting the retina and producing a visual sensation. The visible portion of the electromagnetic spectrum extends from about 380 to 770 nm.

Load-bearing: A wall that is capable of bearing another weight as well as its own.

Lock: A contrivance for fastening and unfastening at will a door, casement, chest, drawer, or the like, usually one of which the essential part is a bolt shot and withdrawn by means of a removable key. Door locks have usually a Latch as well as the bolt moved by the key. Locks for safes and strong rooms are sometimes of extraordinary complication, and many rival inventions have at different times demanded the attention of builders, resulting in a system of defence against theft, which amounts almost to perfect security so far as the lock is concerned. Locks of this sort sometimes shoot bolts in all four directions, and are frequently operated without keys, thus avoiding the necessity of a keyhole into which an explosive may be forced.

Lodge: A mason's workshop within a medieval church or castle during construction.

Log Construction: A building made of hewn or raw logs notched and stacked to form walls often filled with mud or mortar between the cracks.

Loggia: In Italian architecture, a roofed structure open on at least one side and affording a protected sitting place out of doors; commonly a prominent part of a building and forming a porch or gallery, but not infrequently an independent structure serving as a public shelter. The loggia is a frequent and important feature of the architecture of the Italian palazzi, and, less frequently, of the public buildings and open squares; but the term is hardly to be used in connection with such colonnades and like structures as are intended to serve certain positive purposes, e.g. an ambulatory, or covered passageway. In its application to private residences, it corresponds very closely to the veranda of the country houses of the United States; but the word, in its adopted English sense, is restricted to mean a subordinate, partially enclosed space forming a room open to the air, but still contained within the body of the building.

Lumber: In the United States, in connection with building and manufacturing, wood as prepared for the market; whether in the log or in sawed or more elaborately dressed pieces. In Great Britain, such material is known simply as wood. As usually prepared for building purposes, lumber intended for the rougher operations of framing and the like is squared from the log in sawmills according to standard dimensions, but is otherwise undressed; while the lighter material, as for sheathing, ceiling, and other finish is commonly

planed on one face and perhaps
slightly molded, as with a tongue
and groove, a bead, or the like. The
British system of classifying wood
under definite names, according to
its dimensions, is quite unknown in
the United States, except in a very
general way. Thus, squared pieces
for framing and the like are
commonly all designated as
Scantling when not more than about
30 square inches in cross section;
pieces of larger size being known as
Timber, with or without the article.
Thus, a piece 5" x 6" in size has been
in the lumber trade more or less
officially defined as a Scantling; a
piece of 6" x 6" as a Dimension
Timber. It is, therefore, in the
United States, quite common to
designate lumber by the use for
which any given size may be
primarily designed, as Studding,
Furring, Sheathing, Veneer.

M

Machicolation: A castle tower gallery projection from brackets. Used for dropping hot oil or projection missiles.

Mansard: In French, a dormer window. A term derived from Mansard or Mansart, the name or surname of several architects. The French term is extended to a roof lighted by such windows *comble a la Mansard* and to the chambers within; in this sense expressing the same idea as the English Garret, a humble lodging in the roof.

Mantel: (A) A projecting hood or cover above a fireplace to collect the smoke and guide it into the chimney flue above (B) Same as Mantelpiece; a modern abbreviation.

Mantelpiece: A structure forming a mantel, together with its supports; a similar structure built against a chimney around and above a fireplace, either as a decorative finish or to afford one or more shelves above the fireplace.

Maqsura: A wooden screen in a mosque designed to protect the ruler from a crowd. The detached part of a mosque used for prayer.

Marble: Any stone consisting essentially or carbonate of lime, or the carbonates of lime and magnesia, and of such color and texture as to make it desirable for the higher grades of building, monumental, or decorative work. The varying shades of gray and the black colors of marbles are due to the presence of carbonaceous matter; the yellow, brown and red colors to iron oxides, and the green to the presence of silicate minerals, as mica and talc. The veined and clouded effects are due to an unequal distribution of the coloring constituents throughout the mass of the stone.

Martello Tower: A round low guntower.

Mason's Mark: The signature or mark of the mason who executed a building. Common on Gothic and Romanesque buildings.

Masonry: The art and practice of building with stone, natural or artificial, with brick, and, by extension, with molded earth, as in adobe and pise; also, the work so produced. Stones and bricks are generally laid in mortar, but may be laid without it (dry masonry), care being taken so to superimpose the materials as to bind or bond together those below them.

Megalith: A large stone block. Usually undressed or roughly dressed. For example, the stones of Stonehenge.

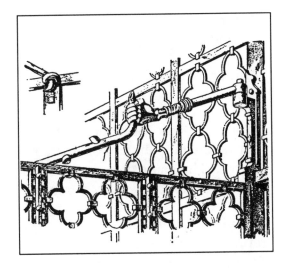

Metal Work: (A) Work done by melting metal and molding or casting it in forms which can then be more or less finished by hand, as with cutting tools and files. (B) Work done by hammering and beating into shape metal either hot or cold. The decoration of metal by means of inlay of different kinds is reducible to one of the two systems above named, except where it is a result of engraving, as in

damascened work; but such ornamentation as this hardly enters into architectural practice of any period. The soldering of small parts together is common in jewellery, but only in rare cases in connection with building. The use of wire concerns only lathing and such simple railing as is used temporarily or in slight structures. Engraving upon metal is used in what is known as the Memorial Brass, and the engraved lines were filled with some colored material. Enamelling is used upon tombs, but chiefly in details of heraldry or of the costume of portrait statues. The ornamental metal work of architecture proper is generally confined to bronze, which comes under definition A, and wrought iron, which comes under definition B. These will be treated below. Cast-iron is hardly to be recognized as of decorative value.

Metope: In a Doric entablature, that part of the front which is interposed between two triglyphs. The term implies, etymologically, the space between the triglyphs, whether open or closed; but in architecture it is applied almost exclusively to the slab or block of stone which fills this space, and this because we have no Grecian monument in which metopes have been left open. That they were so in early times appears from several passages in Greek literature. The metopes, considered as blocks of marble, were made the medium for very elaborate sculpture and painted decoration, and that from an early time. The painted metopes have generally lost their decoration to such an extent that they are no longer easily understood. As the metope was of necessity a nearly square tablet, without constructional utility, it became natural to use an elaborate kind of sculpture for its decoration. Thus, in the Parthenon, the very highest relief is used--relief so high that the heads and limbs are sometimes detached from the background. The theme, or artistic subject, of each metope is generally limited to its own small surface, and a certain monotony of treatment follows the constant repetition of bodies of centaurs and warriors in violent action, or, as on the east front of the Thescion, the labors of Hercules.

Meurtriere: A small loophole in a fort or military structure sized for a musket or gun barrel.

Mews: Stables with living quarters behind a London town-house. The cul de sac leading to a mews.

Mezzanine: A small floor that is between two main floors.

Mihrab: A niche for prayer in a mosque.

Minaret: A tall tower connected to a mosque.

Minbar: The high pulpit in a mosque.

Minster: Medieval name for a monastic establishment or related church. The name of certain English and European cathedral churches.

Minute: The unit of measure representing one sixtieth of the diameter of a classical column at the base of the shaft.

Misericord: The bracket on the underside of the seat of a hinged choir stall which serves as a seat or rest during choir.

Modular Design: A design based on fixed modules. Prefabricated or industrialized building or construction.

Module: A standard, usually of length, by which the proportionate measurements of a building are supposed to be determined. Vitruvius says that the front of a Doric building, if columnar, is, when tetrastyle, to be divided into twenty-eight parts; if hexastyle, into forty-four parts; and that each of these parts is a "modulus," called by the Greeks embates. He says, farther, that the thickness of a column (shaft) should be two moduli, the height with the capital, fourteen, the height of the capital alone, one module, and its width one and one-sixth; and he applies similar rules to the entablature. Starting from these loosely written chapters, which even its author could hardly have thought authoritative, or even exact, the writers of the Italian Renaissance and their imitators have laid down exact proportionate measurements for all parts of the order, dividing the module into parts called minutes, in English, twelve, eighteen, or thirty of them to a module; and taking the module itself, now a semidiameter, now a whole diameter, now the third of a diameter, now a fraction of the height of a column.

Modulus: (A) A unit of measure assumed in determining the strength of materials as against stretching, bending, or rupture. (B) Same as module.

Mold: (A) A form used to guide a workman, whether a solid object requiring to be exactly copied or reproduced by casting, or a profile cut out of a board or piece of sheet metal. In the second of these characters the mold is used for running plaster moldings and the like. (B) The hollow into which melted metal, liquid plaster, or the like is poured in the process of casting. Such a mold is itself a direct case or impression of a mold in sense A. (C) Same as molding; a common abbreviation used by the trades in composition, as bed mold.

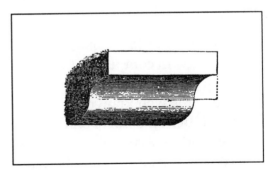

Molding: (A) The plane, curved, broken, irregular, or compound surface formed at the face of any piece or member by casting, cutting, or otherwise shaping and modelling the material, so as to produce modulations of light, shade, and shadow. The term is generally understood as meaning such a surface when continued uniformly to a considerable extent, as a continuous band or a series of small parts. (B) By extension, a piece of material worked with a molding or group of moldings, in sense A, on one or more sides; the piece being usually just large enough to receive the molding so worked and to afford one or two plane surfaces by which it is secured in place for decorative or other purpose. (C) From the common use of wooden moldings made separate and very cheaply, in the molding mill, any slender strip of material planed and finished, used for covering joints, concealing wires, and the like.

Moment of Inertia: A quantity in constant use in computing the strength and deflection of a beam or column. It is well known that when a beam is bent the fibers on the concave side are compressed, and on the convex side, extended, though all are not equally extended or compressed. If we suppose the section of a beam or of a column to be divided into infinitely small areas, and each area multiplied by the square of its distance from a line passing through the center of gravity of the section, the sum of these products is the moment of inertia of the section, and, when multiplied by the strength of the fiber, represents the sum of the resistance of the different fibres to stress. The square of the radius of gyration r^2 is the moment of inertia, divided by the area of the section. It is the sum of the squares of the distances of the small areas from the axis about which the moment is taken. If we represent each of these small areas by a, and the variable distance of each area from the center line, or axis, by y, then the moment of inertia, $I=ay^2$, the sum of the small areas each by the square of y (meaning "sum"). But the sum of the small areas equals A, the whole area of the section. If we call the sum of all the values of y^2, r^2, then $I=Ar^2$, which gives $[I}=r^2$, or the radius of gyration, $r=[]$.

Monolith: A single stone used as a monument.

Monopteral: A building with a single row of columns on all sides.

Moon gate: A circular opening used in Chinese architecture instead of a door.

Mortar: A mixture of lime or of cement, or of both, with sand and water, or, of those materials with some other, such as plaster of Paris. Ordinary mortar is made with lime and sand alone; that made with cement is generally called cement mortar, and that with plaster of Paris is called gauge mortar. By extension, bitumen, Nile mud, adobe clay, etc., are called by this name.

The use of mortar in building is not primarily to act as an adhesive mixture and to hold two masses of stone, brick, or the like together, but to interpose its soft and yielding, but soon hardening, mass between courses of stone or brick, and thus enable the uppermost one to take a more perfect bearing or bed upon the surface below. Its secondary purpose is to afford an artificial matrix, in which small materials may be so bedded that, when the whole mass of mortar is hardened, the wall, pier, or the like forms a solid homogeneous mass. This object is gained in one of two ways; first, by laying the mortar in quantity upon the upper surface of the masonry already completed and bedding the bricks or small stones upon it while it is still soft; second, by mingling the mortar with the small materials, as broken stone, brick, and the like, and throwing the whole mass together into the place to be filled by it.

The Greeks seem not to have used mortar after the Mycenaen period. The temples which we admire were built entirely of solid blocks of stone fitted one upon another with dry beds, the surfaces being made to correspond accurately; in some cases, at least, by grinding one upon the other. Among the Romans, in the immense works carried out by the engineers of the Empire, mortar was unknown in cut-stone walling, and even in vaulting when composed of large blocks of stone; but the great masses of Roman vaulting, walling, etc., after the time of Augustus, were commonly built of small roughly shaped blocks of stone bedded in quantities of strong cement mortar, and the whole surface faced with flat, thin bricks or tiles.

Wherever brickwork was used in antiquity it was of necessity used with some adhesive material; thus, even the Egyptians of very early time used Nile mud, and the builders of Mesopotamia used bitumen (called slime in Genesis), although the unbaked bricks most in use in this region were cemented together by the powdered clay of which they were made, mixed with water and with a little chopped straw.

Mortar in the strict sense was not in use in this early time; even the Mycenaean Greeks seem to have used only soft bituminous clay to close the open joints of rough stone work. Since the fall of the great Roman Empire, building has been commonly done with mortar, whether the chief material is cut stone, rough stone, or brick. The vaults of the earlier Middle Ages were built of rubble stone made to adhere by mortar used in great abundance, and the thick walls of that time had little coherence except that afforded by the mortar in which the stones were bedded. In modern bricklaying, mortar serves almost exactly the same purpose. The brick-layer spreads the mortar in a thick bed upon the surface below, and lays half a dozen bricks rapidly upon this mortar, forcing the soft material upward in the vertical joints as he does so.

One of the chief requirements in good brickwork, and which distinguishes it from inferior work of the same kind, is the use of mortar in great abundance, gilling up the whole of the solid mass, and not allowing irregular openings, large or small, between its two faces.

Mote-and-Bailey: A Norman defense system made up of an earth mound with a wooden tower and surrounded by a bailey.

Mote: A steep mound associated with eleventh and twelfth century castles.

Mounting height: When specifying or installing an item, unless noted otherwise, it is the distance from the floor to the top edge or surface of the object.

Mullion: A slender, vertical, intermediate member forming part of a framework, or serving to subdivide an opening or the like. The term is, perhaps, to be considered as referring to an accessory piece introduced for ornament or for some subordinate purpose, rather than to a supporting member forming part of the general construction. The strips of wood or another material that divide a window into two or more sections.

Muntin: A small, slender mullion in light framing, as a sash bar, a middle stile of a door. The vertical part in a door or window frame which butts into the horizontal rails. A sash bar.

Muttule: The square block projecting above a triglyph and under a corona on a Doric cornice.

N

Nail: A slender and small piece of material, usually metal, intended to be driven into anything, especially a board, plank, joist, or other wooden member, for the purpose of holding fast, usually by the elastic force of the wood pressing against it. The term is usually confined to the above described form, but in composition (as in Tree Nail or Trenail) a different signification is implied, which does not generally concern the architect or builder.

Naos: The principal sanctuary or chamber in a Greek temple which contained the statue of the god.

Narthex: An enclosure at the main entrance of a church. The transverse vestibule preceding the nave and aisles as an inner narthex or preceding the facade as an outer narthex.

Nave: The middle section of a church, the lengthwise section between the aisles.

Nebule: A molding with a serpentine or wavy lower edge.

Necking: The narrow molding around the bottom of a capital.

Niche: An indentation in a wall to hold a vase or other decorations.

Nonbearing wall: A non-structural wall or partition.

O

Obelisk: A tapering shaft with a rectangular section and ending in a pyramid. Often made of monolithic stone and serving as a monument or as a small decorative *objet d'art*.

Octagon: An eight equally-sided figure often used as a ground-plan in classical and subsequent architecture.

Octastyle: In the style of a portico with eight frontal columns.

Oculus: A circular opening in a ceiling or wall. Usually opening onto a hemisphere or dome.

Oeillet: A small opening in a medieval fortification used for launching projectiles.

Off-set: The part of a wall which is horizontally exposed when the portion above is reduced in thickness.

Offices: Buildings only for professional use and are not used for any living purposes.

Ogee: A double-curved line consisting of a convex and concave part. A fourteenth century molding in the shape of an *S*.

Onion Dome: A bulbous pointed, onion shaped dome common on Eastern European churches.

Opisthodomos: The enclosed rear section of a Greek temple. The treasury.

Opus Alexandrinum: Decorative paving made-up of mosaic and opus sectile in guilloche design.

Opus Incertum: A Roman wall made with a concrete face and irregularly shaped stones.

Opus Listatum: A Roman wall with alternating brick and stone block courses.

Opus Quadratum: A Roman wall made of squared stones.

Opus Reticulatum: A Roman wall of concrete with diagonally spaced squared stones in the pattern of a net.

Opus Sectile: Decorative paving of geometric marble slabs.

Orangery: A garden building for growing oranges. A green-house or hot-house which has a window on either side and was developed in the seventeenth century.

Oratory: Private home or church chapel.

Orders of architecture: The orders of architecture consist of three Greek modes and five Roman modes.

Oriel window: See bay window.

Orientation: The siting of a building in relationship to the sun.

Oubliette: A secret medieval prison cell accessed through a trapdoor.

Oversailing Courses: A series of masonry courses each projecting beyond the one below.

P

Pagoda: A Buddhist temple shaped as a polygonal tower with multiple, stacked roofs.

Paint: A liquid solution that has a pigment mixed into another solution such as, water, oil, or an organic solvent.

Pantile: An s-shaped section, roofing tile.

Paradise: An atrium in front of a church. Usually surrounded by a portico.

Parapet: A low wall around the roof of a building or around a drop. Intended for protection. A railing that acts as a firebreak to a roof or ceiling.

Parclose: A chapel screen separating it from the main church.

Parekklesion: A Byzantine chapel.

Parlor: The primary room for entertaining guests and until the twentieth century considered a living room.

Parpen: A stone that passes through a wall with two smooth vertical faces.

Parquet: Thin hardwood, usually of fancy hardwood, flooring laid in patterns. It is often inlaid and highly polished.

Parterre: The part of a theater or auditorium on the ground floor behind the orchestra. A level space in a garden, next to the main house.

Parvis: (French) Open space in front of or around churches and cathedrals.

Pastophory: An Early Christian church room which serves as a prothesis.

Pavilion: An exhibition hall or sports hall. A projected attachment to a larger building. An ornamental building with no particular utility.

Pediment: A low-pitched gable above a portico.

Pencil pointer: A drafting tool to sharpen the point of drafting lead. The basic type with steel cutter is recommended over other types. It has several bushings for different pencil diameters, and has a gauge for blunt or sharp cutting. A sand-paper board is good for rendering and sketching. It can chisel and blunt leads for special techniques.

Pendientive: A spandrel that is concave and leads from the angle of two walls to the base of a circular dome.

Penthouse: The top floor of an office or residential building, usually a living space. A subsidiary structure on top of another structure with a lean-to or other separate roof.

Pergola: A covered garden walk often formed by a double row of pillars supporting beams.

Peristyle: A range of columns surrounding a building or court.

Perron: A flight of steps ascending to a platform. An exterior platform accessed by steps at the entrance of a building.

Piano Nobile: The main floor of a house with public spaces.

Piazza: An open space surrounded by buildings. A long walk covered by a roof supported by columns.

Picture Plane: The two-dimension plane that the observer sees through.

It is perpendicular to the observer's sight line and all lines from the observer to the object cross through it.

Pier, Buttress: (A) A pier which serves as a buttress while having another purpose, as when a pier dividing openings in an outer wall receives also the thrust of a vault within and is, therefore, shaped so as to resist that thrust. One such, in a gallery near the church of S. Pietro in Perugia, is the corner pier of a building with arches of the outer wall thrusting against it on two sides, and a groin vault within thrusting against it in a diagonal direction; to meet all of these thrusts the pier is greatly widened at the base and has a continuous batter on two sides. In the Chapel of Henry VII in Westminister Abbey the massive piers of the rounded apse, whose axes radiate from the center of the curve, are buttress piers; and so are the massive octagonal shafts along the north and south sides; that is to say, they are primarily piers of vertical support and of an architectural design agreeing with that function; but they also act as buttresses to take up the thrust of the aisle vaulting. (B) That part of a buttress which rises above the point of thrust of a vault which it is intended to maintain, or above the roof of the building to which it is attached. Thus, in Gothic construction, the prismatic pier which rises above the aisle roof and takes the thrust of the flying buttress is sometimes called by this name. Such piers often are carried up vertically on the outer side; but on the inner side, toward the flying buttress, are built overhanging or corbelled inward, so that the thrust from within is partly counterbalanced by the tendency of the unsymmetrical pier to fall inward.

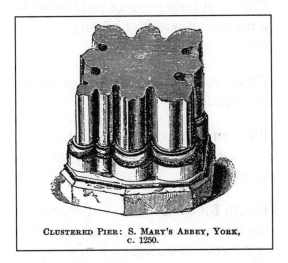

CLUSTERED PIER: S. MARY'S ABBEY, YORK, c. 1250.

Pier: A solid masonry support. The solid mass between windows and doors and other openings in the building.

Pigment: Highly colored insoluble powdered substance used to impart color to other materials. White pigments, e.g., titanium dioxide, are dispersed in fiber forming polymers to produce delustered (semidull and dull) fibers.

PILLAR: NAVE ARCADE PIERS IN THE FORM OF SIMPLE PILLARS; FOUNTAINS ABBEY, YORKSHIRE, ENGLAND; c. 1180.

Pier, Clustered: See compound pier.

Pier, Compound: A pier with multiple shafts.

Pillar: A free-standing member of any shape as opposed to a column which conforms to a classical shape.

Pilotis: (French) Pillars that support a building raising it above the ground to second story level.

Pinnacle: A steep conical or pyramidal finial or ornamentation.

Piscina: A shallow basin or sink, supplied with a drain pipe, generally recessed in a niche, which is often elaborately decorated. In churches, generally situated in a canopied niche in the sanctuary wall, on the Epistle, or south side of the altar, and east of the Sedelia, used to receive the water in which the priest washes his hands at the Mass, and also that in which the sacred vessels are cleaned.

Plaisance: A summerhouse near a mansion.

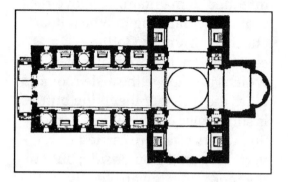

Plan: The horizontal design or arrangement of building parts as well as the drawing that represents it.

Plank: A long piece of lumber with a minimum width of twenty centimeters.

Plate: A covering for exterior nails and studs.

Plenum: A space that is under the roof and above the ceiling used for conduits.

Plinth Block: A block which stops the wall skirting at the base of a door or other architectural feature.

Plinth: The base of a column or doorway also a support for sculpture.

Plumb: Exactly vertical.

Plywood: A panel composed of a crossbanded assembly of layers or plies of veneer, or veneers in combination with a lumber core or particleboard core, that are joined with an adhesive. Except for special constructions, the grain of alternate plies is always approximately at right angles, and the thickness and species on either side of the core are identical for balanced effect. An odd number of plies is always used.

Podium: A speakers platform. The arena platform in an amphitheater. A continuous base supporting columns.

Point-Block Housing: A high block which reserves the center for staircases and elevators. Suites or apartments radiate from the center.

Pointing: The exposed mortar finishing to masonry joints raked out with a trowel to receive it.

Pool: A basin filled with water and used for swimming.

Porch: The covered entrance to a building.

Portcullis: An iron gate which slides vertically in grooves made in the doorway jambs. Used in castles and forts.

Porte-cochere: A covered driveway associated with an office building, hotel, etc.

Portico: A porch supported by columns. A roofed space forming the entrance of a building.

Post-and-beam: A construction system with horizontal beams and vertical posts.

Posts: Vertical timbers which carry longitudinal roof members. Main vertical wall timbers. Small metal or wood columns.

Prefabrication: Manufacturing of building components prior to assembly into a building.

Presbytery: The part of a church reserved for the priest, often east of the choir. The site of the high altar.

Principals: A pair of vertically inclined timbers of a truss which carry common rafters.

Profile: A molding section or contour. The outline of an object or building.

Pronaos: The vestibule of a Greek or Roman temple.

Propylaeum: The gateway to an enclosure.

Proscenium: The wall in a theatre which divides the stage from the orchestra. The proscenium opening is usually framed with an arch and covered by a curtain. The stage on which the action in a Greek or Roman theatre took place.

Prothesis: The room used in an Orthodox or Byzantine church to prepare the sacraments. A sacristy.

Pseudo-dipteral: A classical temple planed as a dipteral but without the inner column range.

Pseudo-peripteral: A classical temple with porticos at either end and with columns or pilaster at the sides.

Pteroma: The space in a Greek temple between the walls and colonnades.

Pulpit: The preaching platform or lectern in a church.

Pulpitum: A stone screen in a large church separating the nave from the choir.

Pulvin: A dosseret above the capital supporting the arch above in Byzantine architecture.

Pulvinated: Convex in profile.

Purlin: A horizontal longitudinal timber. A piece of timber that rests between a joist and a rafter.

Putlock: Holes in a wall used to support scaffolding during construction.

Pycnostyle: An arrangement of columns set 1.5 times their diameter apart.

Pylon: A high isolated structure used to mark a boundary or for decoration. A pyramidal tower which flanks an ancient Egyptian temple gateway.

Q

Quadrangle: A rectangular courtyard or mall surrounded by buildings.

Quarry: A small diamond-shaped pane. Used to glaze medieval leaded windows. A small quadrangular opening in window tracery.

Queen-post: A pair of vertical timbers placed symmetrically on a tie-beam and supporting side purlings.

Quirk: A sharp v-shaped cut in or between moldings.

Quoin: (A) One stone helping to form the corner of a wall of masonry, especially when accentuated by a difference in the surface treatment of the stones forming the corner from that of the rest of the wall mass; one of the stones forming such a corner. (B) A wedge to support and steady a stone; a pinner.

Quoins: Alternating large and small dressed stones at the corners of buildings.

R

Rafter: A roof beam; one of those which are set sloping, the lower end bearing on the wall plate, the upper end on the ridge piece or its equivalent.

Rafters: Inclined lateral timbers sloping from wall-top to apex and supporting the roof covering.

Raggle: A masonry groove cut in masonry to receive a roof edge.

Rail: A horizontal member in a door or window frame or panel. In carpentry, any horizontal member mortised or otherwise secured between or upon two posts, forming a frame or panel, as, first, in fencing, whether the closure is made by several parallel rails or by only two to give nailing to palings; second, as a coping to a balustrade, when it is called a hand rail; third, in panelling, doors, and the like, being the horizontal member of the frame in which the panels are set, the vertical members being the stiles. The rails of massive stone, elaborately sculptured, which form the ceremonial enclosures of ancient Buddhist topes, temples, etc., in India, are among the most characteristic and important features of Buddhist architecture.

Railing: Primarily, any structure or member composed mainly of rails; in common use, a parapet, enclosure or the like made with slender bars and of no great size. Such a parapet, whether consisting of balusters or of a trellis of wire or laths, or of iron bars equal or nearly so in thickness, or parallel or nearly so, is called a railing, but the term does not commonly include balustrades or the like of stone.

Rainwater Head: A metal structure used to collect water from a gutter and discharge it into a down-pipe.

Rake: Inclination or slope, as of a roof or of a flight of steps in a staircase.

Rampart: A defensive wall surrounding a castle or fort. Usually made from stone or earth.

Random Ashlar: Masonry made of rectangular stones set without continuous joints.

Ravelin: A military outwork made up of two angular faces and constructed in front of the curtain wall.

Rear Vault: A vaulted space between window glass and the inner face of a wall.

Regulus: The short band on a Doric entablature between the tenia and guttae.

Reinforced brick masonry: Masonry that has steel inside the brick to reinforce it.

Reinforced Concrete: Concrete that has been reinforced by insertion of steel mesh or rods. This increases the tensile strength of the material which is inherently strong in compression and weak in tension.

Relief: That which is raised or embossed on a more or less uniform surface; raised work. A bold embossing is called high relief, *alto rilievo*; a low embossing is called low relief, or bas-relief, *basso rilievo*; a middle or half-relief is called *mezzo relievo*. In high relief the figures or objects represented project at least one half their natural rotundity or circumference from the back ground, parts of the figures sometimes being undercut and solid like statues, as in pediment sculpture; in low relief the projection of the figures is but slight, no part being entirely detached; a very flat relief, such as is seen on some coins, is called *stiacciato rilievo*. An Egyptian form of relief is counter sunk, i.e. it does not project above the general surface upon which it is wrought. This is known as *cavo rilievo* or *intaglio rilevato*; also hollow relief or coelanaglyphic sculpture. The outlines are incised, and the relief is thus contained in a sunk panel no bigger than itself. Relief work executed in thin metal may be done by repousse work, or by chasing; or may be copied by the electrotype process. Other relief in metal is done by casting. Relief work of the best periods did not represent its subject pictorially, and the surface upon which subject and action were depicted was recognized as the actual background, no attempt having been made at perspective illusions. But in later art, this proper condition of relief work was less uniformly respected, and as in the panels of the arch of Titus, and in those of the bronze gates of the Baptistry at Pisa, actual pictorial subjects were attempted with distant backgrounds.

Relieve: To assist any overloaded member by any device of construction, as, in the case of a lintel, by building over it a discharging or relieving arch to transfer the burden to the piers or beams of iron or steel to receive the imposed weight, or by placing between the lintel and the supporting pier a bolster or raising piece, or by the use of a brace, etc.; or, in the case of a pier or section of wall, to spread the weight of a girder or beam bearing upon it over a larger surface by interposing a plate of metal or wood; or, in the case of a beam or girder in wood construction, bearing a wooden partition or any portion of the frame, to build in the partition or frame a truss with suspension rods or suspension timbers to transfer the weight to the piers or walls; or, in the case of the soil under a foundation pier, to ease it from the great concentration of burden by broad levellers of stone or concrete, by inverted arches connected with other piers, etc.

Remodeling: A construction project of revising the existing structure.

Render: (A) In building, to apply plaster directly to brickwork, stonework, tiles, or slate; said especially of the first coat, the application of the final coat being described by the term *to set,* and an intermediate, when used, by *to float.* Two coat work is hence often called render and set, or render set work; while three coat is known as render float and set. (B) In drawing, to give to a mechanical drawing, as an elevation, a more or less complete indication of shades and shadows, whether in ink, color, or other medium.

Reredos: A wooden, metal or stone wall or screen behind an altar.

Resistance: (A) The power of any substance, as building material, to resist forces, such as Compression, Cross Breaking, Shear, Tension, Torsion. (B) In HVAC, thermal conduction reciprocal.

Reveal: That portion of the jamb of an opening or recess which is visible from the face of the wall back to the frame or other structure which may be placed between the jambs. Thus, the windows of an ordinary brick building have usually reveals of some four inches; that being the width of each brick jamb visible outside of the window frames.

Reverse Ogee Molding: A double curved molding: it is convex above and concave below.

Revetment: Marble or other facing applied to a ball made of another material.

Rib: A molding on an arched or flat ceiling; but specifically and more properly, in medieval vaulting, an arch, generally molded, forming part of the skeleton upon which rest the intermediate concave surfaces which constitute the shell or closure of the vault. The crowning intersections of these arches or ribs are adorned with sculptured bosses. In quadripartite vaulting the main diagonal ribs called by that name and also arcs ogives; each transverse rib is called arc doubleau, and each longitudinal rib, are formed. To this fundamental system of ribs supplementary and subordinate ribs were afterward added, dividing the concave of the ceiling into many panels, but in general these had no function in the construction.

Rise: (A) The vertical distance between two consecutive treads in a stair; sometimes, the entire height of a flight of stairs from landing to landing. (B) The vertical height of the curved part of an arch, that is the distance measured vertically, as in an elevation, from the springing line to the highest point of the curved intrados.

Riser: (A) The upright of one step, whether the step be in one piece as a block of stone, or built up. In the former case, the riser is the surface along. In the latter case, the riser is the board, plate of cast iron, or similar thin piece which is set upright between two treads. (B) By extension, the same as Rise. A stair in which the treads are separate planks, slabs or slate, plates or iron, or the like, is sometimes built without risers. In this case, an incorrect extension of the term is used, and such a stair is said to have open risers.

Roll: (A) A nearly cylindrical member, comparatively small, especially a rounded strip of wood fastened to and continuous with a ridge or hip of a roof; a false ridge pole. (B) In a roof of lead or other metal, one of a series of rounded strips of wood secured at regular intervals along the slope, and extending from the ridge to the eaves, over which the ends of the roofing plates are turned and lapped, thus preventing the crawling of the metal by alternate expansion and contraction. (C) A similar rounded piece made by the metal sheathing along, or with the support of a wooden batten.

Roman Order: The peculiar system introduced by the Romans of late Republican or early Imperial times, by which an arched construction is given some appearance of Greek post-and-lintel building. In the illustration under Alette, in each story an engaged column carries, in appearance, an entablature. The abutments and the arch which they carry, and the wall upon this arch, are, however, the real structure, and the entablature is merely an ornamental balcony. The structure is really a highly adorned arcade.

Rood Loft: A gallery above a rood screen to contain images or candles.

Rood Screen: A screen below the rood.

Rood: A cross or crucifix.

Roof, Barrel: (A) Same as Barrel Vault. (B) A roof or ceiling which has within the appearance of a Barrel Vault; a ceiling of nearly semicircular section.

Roof, Belfast: See Roof, bowstring.

Roof, Bowstring: A roof constructed with curved timber truss and horizontal tie-beams connected by diagonal wood latices.

Roof, Common rafter: A roof in which pairs of rafters are not connected by a collar-beam.

Roof, Compass: See Roof, cradle.

Roof, Coupled: A ridged or double pitched roof of the simplest construction, often without tiebeam or collar beam, depending upon the stiffness of the walls for its permanence, and, therefore, of small span.

Roof, Coupled rafter: A roof in which the rafters are connected by collar-beams.

Roof Covering: The closure laid upon a roof frame, including the wood sheathing or boarding, and the outside protection or weathering by metal, slate, tiles, shingles, painted canvas, tarred paper, thatch, by any composition of tar, bitumen, asphaltum, etc., with gravel, or any other form of protection against the weather. In the few cases of absolutely incombustible construction the slates or tiles are tied by lead wire to iron laths; or, the roof being filled up solid with brick, terra cotta, or cement blocks, large sheets of copper, zinc, or lead may be nailed upon it, lapping over one another like slates, and left free at the lower end to allow for expansion and contraction; or, in flat roofs, large slabs of slate or stone are bedded in cement. In the more usual cases, roofs of any pitch may be covered with metal, which is nearly always of tin plates in the United States; though term plates are used, and, much more rarely, zinc, as in France, lead, as often in Great Britain, or copper. The term, The Leads, applied in England to a nearly flat roof which may be used as a floor, is unknown in the United States, where such a roof would be covered with tin plates or tar and gravel. Steep roofs alone may be covered with tiles, slate, or shingles, laid in the usual way, without any filling or cementing of the joints; and it is to be noted that rain and snow may beat in through the crevices to a slight degree without serious damage.

Roof, Cradle: A form of timber roof much used in the Middle Ages for churches and large halls, in which the rafters, collar beams, and braces of each truss were combined into an approximately arched form, and sometimes indeed had their soffits cut to the curve of an arch, producing internally the effect of a series of arches; or, when the arched members were ceiled, of a cradle vault.

Roof, Curb: One in which the slope is broken on two or four sides; so called because a horizontal curb is built at the plane where the slope changes.

Roof, Double-framed: A roof constructed with longitudinal members such as purlins.

Roof, Flat: (A) One whose surface is actually horizontal or with no perceptible slope, as in the mud, earth, or cement roofs of tropical countries and the roofs of brick or terra cotta supported by iron beams and covered with water-tight material which are characteristic of modern fireproof buildings. (B) A roof having a slope so slight that one can walk or sit upon it as upon a floor. Of this kind are the metal-covered roofs of Europe and America in which the slope is often half an inch to a foot or one in twenty-four. The plates of metal in these cases must be soldered together with care.

Roof, French: A curb roof with sides set at a very steep angle so as sometimes to approach verticality, while the top above the curb may be nearly flat or may have a visible slope though much less steep than the lower slope. The term is of United States origin, and applies especially to a form of roof which, beginning about 1865, became very common all over the country.

Roof, Gable; Gabled: A ridge roof which terminates at each end in a gable, as distinguished from a hipped roof. A gambrel roof is a form of gable roof.

Roof, Gambrel: A curb roof with only the two opposite sides sloping; it is therefore a gabled curb roof. This form is common throughout New England, New Jersey and eastern New York, having been adopted by the earlier colonists of the northern states, and being much more frequently seen there than in the countries whence the colonists came.

Roof, Helm: A roof with four inclined faces joined at the top, with a gable at each foot.

Roof, Hip; Hipped: One having hips by which the projecting angles between two adjacent slopes are squared. Thus, a pyramidal roof is one which has four hips; and in some cases a roof, as on a building or irregular plan, may have more hips than four and often alternating with valleys.

Roof, Homogeneous: One in which the same mass of material furnished the outer pitch for shedding rain water and the surface exposed within; that is to say, a roof forming a solid shell either of compact masonry, as often in Byzantine art, or of slabs of stone, as in Syria and in a few churches of Europe.

Roof, Hyperbolic Paraboloid: A roof structure in the shape of a geometerical form made of double curved shell generated by straight lines.

Roof, Jerkin Head: A ridge roof of which the ridge is shorter than the eaves, having two gables, each of which is truncated halfway up or thereabout so that the roof is hipped above. it may be otherwise explained as a hipped roof, of which the hips starting from the ridge are too short to reach the eaves, so that the roof below becomes a gabled roof of which the gables are truncated.

Roof, Lean-to: One with a single slope; as where the aisle of a church is usually roofed with a single slope from the wall of the clearstory outward.

Roof, M: One in which two ridges parallel or nearly so to one another are separated by a receding or dropping valley, gutter, or the like; a device sometimes resorted to for diminishing the height of the roof, as in supposed necessities of the architectural style, and sometimes resulting from the building of an addition when it is not desired to disturb the earlier roof.

Roof, Mansard: A curbed roof with dormer windows of some size; that is to say, such a roof as will best provide for habitable rooms within it. This is the roof common in neoclassic and modern *chateaux* and public buildings in France, the deck or upper slope being usually small in proportion to the lower slopes, whereas in the French roof the reverse may be the case.

Roof, Pavilion: A roof hipped on all sides so as to have a pyramidal or nearly pyramidal form.

Roof, Penthouse: A roof with one pitch like that of a shed or of the aisle of a church in the ordinary distribution.

Roof, Pitched: A sloped roof with gable ends.

Roof, Pyramidal: One in the form of a pyramid or, by extension, a hipped roof in which the ridge is relatively short so that the sloping sides end nearly in a point.

Roof, Ridge; Ridged: A double pitched roof, the two slopes of which meet at a horizontal ridge.

Roof, Saddleback: A gable roof in some peculiar position, as when a tower is roofed in this way instead of terminating in a flat terrace or in a spire.

Roof, Shed: Same as Penthouse Roof.

Roof, Single-framed: A roof framed without trusses, the opposite rafters being tied together by the upper floor frame or by boards nailed across horizontally to serve as ties or collars.

Roof, Slab Slate: A roof covered with slabs or flags of slate, as in cottages built in the neighborhood of slate quarries.

Roof, Span: A roof composed of two equal slopes, as a nave roof, in contradistinction to one having one slope, as an aisle roof or penthouse roof.

Roof, Terrace: A flat roof, especially when the roofing is of masonry and the surface allows of free use of the roof as a place for walking and taking the air.

Roof, Trough: Same as M Roof.

Roof, Truss: A roof, the rafters of which are supported on a truss, or a series of trusses, by means of purlins.

Roof: That part of the closure of a building which covers it in from the sky. Upon this part of a building depends in large measure the character of its design as a work of architecture. Roofs are distinguished: (1) By their form and method of construction; as, the flat roof, characteristic of dry tropical countries, and much used in modern commercial buildings in the United States; the sloping roof, including gables, hipped, penthouse, mansard, and gambrel roofs with their varieties. (2) By the character of their covering; as, thatched, shingled, battened, slated, tiled, metal-covered, tarred, asphalted, gravelled, etc. (A) In carpentry, the

term refers to the timber framework by which the external surface is supported. This, in sloping roofs, consists usually of a series of pairs of opposite rafters or couples, of which the lower ends are tied together in various ways to prevent spreading; or, where the span is too great for such simple construction and there are no intermediate upright supports, of a series of rafters supported by longitudinal horizontal purlins, which are generally carried on a system of transverse timber frames or trusses, spaced from 8 to 20 feet apart. In modern practice, these trusses are constructed with principal rafters of which the lower opposite ends are tied together by tiebeams hung in the center from a king-post; or, at two points, from queen-posts, from the lower part of these suspension members, braces or struts may be extended to stiffen the principals. To suit various conditions of shape of roof and area to be covered, these typical and elementary forms are, in modern usage, subjected to innumerable structural modifications and extensions. One of the most marked distinctions in the historic styles consists in the pitch or inclination of the roof. Thus in the Greek temple the slope of the pediment varied from 15 degrees to 16 1/2 degrees; Roman roofs had a slope of from 22 degrees to 23 1/2 degrees; Romanesque roofs followed closely the Roman slope; the Gothic pitch was much steeper, sometimes reaching 50 degrees or even 60 degrees. In the Renaissance era there was in Italy a revival of the Roman pitch with the other classic features; but the French builders of this era retained the steepest slopes of the medieval sky lines, especially in the conical roofs of their round towers and in the pyramidal roofs with which they characteristically covered each separate division of their buildings. These lofty roofs, with their high dormers, chimneys, and crestings, constitute a distinctive characteristic of the French Renaissance, the peculiar steep roof being a development from these French traditions. The structural conditions from which the steep mediaeval pitch was evolved.

Roo, Valley: One which covers a building so arranged with projecting wings or pavilions, nearly on the same level as the main roof, that there are valleys at the junction of the two parts of the roof. The term is hardly applied to roofs which have merely the valleys of dormers and small gables.

Room: An enclosure or division of a house or other structure, separated from other divisions by partitions; an apartment, a chamber; as a drawing-room, parlour, dining room, or chamber in a house, a stateroom in a ship or railroad car, a harness room in a stable.

Rotunda: A domed circular building.

Roughing-In: (A) Any coarse mechanical process preliminary and preparatory to final or finished work, as the rough coat of mortar forming a foundation for one or more coats of fine plaster, or, in a scheme of decoration, the necessary mechanical groundwork of colors or modelling. (B) In plumbing, the establishment of the system of pipes for supply and waste, done while the house is preparing for plastering, and before the pipes are connected with the fixtures.

Rubble Masonry: Rough irregular courses of building stones.

S

Sacristy: A church room used to store and prepare vestments and vessels.

Saddle Bars: Small iron bars into which leaded glazed panes are fastened. Used in casement glazing.

Saddle: (A) The cap of a doorsill, or the bottom piece of a door frame, forming a slightly raised ridge, upon which the door, when shut, fits rather closely. The object is to give the under side of the door such height above the floor as to prevent its striking or binding when thrown open. Saddles are made of wood, cast-iron, brass, marble, etc. In England, some carefully built houses have no saddles for the interior doors, the carpets of two adjoining rooms meeting under the doors, the theory being that the floor is so perfectly levelled and built that saddles are unnecessary. (B) Anything used to interpose a vertical support and the foundation or the load upon the support; especially in temporary work, as in Shoring.

Sanctuary: Area around the main altar of a church. In modern use, the

worship space in a church, including the alter, choir and congregational seating spaces.

Scaffold: In building, a temporary wooden framework, put together with nails or ropes, to afford footing for workmen in erecting the walls of a building, or in giving access to ceilings and other parts which cannot be reached from the floors.

Scale rule: A drafting ruler that comes in triangular and flat styles, and in 6" and 12" lengths. 1/4" scale means that a foot in the actual building would be represented by 1/4" on the plan. The scale rule makes thinking in scale much easier, for in the 1/4" scale, the rule is marked just as if each 1/4" is a foot, and these "small" feet are broken into 12 "inches." Other scales like 1/8", 1/4", 1/2", 3/8", 1-1/2", and 3" are represented. A 12" triangular scale rule is the basic scale rule.

Scale: (A) A straight line divided into feet and inches, or meters and centimeters, or the like, according to a definite and stated proportion to reality, as one forty-eight (or four feet to one inch), one one-thousandth, etc. Drawings of all kinds when made by mathematical instruments are made to scale; and the scale may be laid down on the drawing, or may be on a separate piece of paper or wood (see definition B). (B) A rule, generally of metal, ivory, or wood, marked with a scale in sense A, or several such scales, to facilitate the making of drawings and diagrams to any convenient scale. (C) In architectural drawings, the size of the drawings as compared with the actual size of the object delineated, as one-quarter of an inch to the foot. (D) In architectural design, the proportions of a building or its parts, with reference to a definite Module or unit of measurement. (E) A system of proportions to measure the size of a piece of furniture relative to the sizes of the other pieces of furniture in the room.

Scar, Hook butt: One in which the timbers form, in part, butt joints with one or more oblique cuts, by which they are hooked together.

Scarf, end: One formed by the insertion of one end into the other in a manner approaching a mortise and tenon.

Scarf: The oblique joint by which the ends of two pieces of timber are united, long ends of two parts being usually cut with projections and

recesses which mutually fit one another, and these are sometimes forced together and tightened by keys or wedges in various ways, and secured by iron straps and bolts. Also the part cut away and wasted from each timber in shaping it to form this joint.

Schematic: A plan, diagram, or arrangement.

Scotia: Concave molding with a strong shadow cast.

Scratch coat: The first coating of plaster given to a wall.

Screed: (A) A narrow strip of plastering brought to a true surface and edge, or a strip or bar of wood, to guide the workmen in plastering the adjoining section of the wallsurface. (B) A layer of mortar that is applied to concrete for the purpose of laying tiles.

Screen, pardon: A screen surrounding or placed before a confessional, to hide the penitent from public view during the act of confession.

Screen: Any structure of any material having no essential function of support and serving merely to separate, protect, seclude, or conceal. In church architecture, specifically, a decorated pattern of wood, metal, or stone, closed or open, serving to separate, actually or in sentiment, a chapel from the church, an aisle from the nave or choir, the chancel from the nave, etc. In this sense, a screen replaces the Jube in small churches. In early houses of some importance, a partition by which the entrance lobby is separated from the great hall. An open colonnade or arcade if serving to enclose a courtyard, or the like, is sometimes called a screen.

Scribe: To mark with an incised line, as by an awl; hence, to fit one piece to another of irregular or uneven form, as a plain piece against a molded piece, or as in shaping the lower edge of a baseboard to fit the irregularities of the floor.

Section: (A) The surface or portion obtained by a cut made through a structure or any part of one, in such a manner as to reveal its structure and interior detail when the part intervening between the cut and the eye of the observer is removed. (B) The delineation of a section as above defined. In general scale drawings, sections usually represent cuts made through a structure on vertical planes, in contradistinction to cuts made on horizontal planes, which are Plans.

Sedilia: Masonry seats for clergy on the south side of the chancel.

Segment: Section of a circle smaller than a semicircle.

Segmental: A curved member less than a full circle.

Semiarch: An arch of which only one half of its sweep is developed; as in a flying buttress.

Serliana: An archway with three openings, the central one being arched and wider than the others.

Serpentine: (A) An altered rock consisting essentially of a hydrous silicate of magnesia. Used to some extent for building purposes and the finer grades as marble. (B) In the shape of a snake. Complex curves in a decoration or object.

Sewer: A conduit of brickwork, or a vitrified cement or iron pipe channel, intended for the removal of the liquid or semiliquid wastes from habitations, including in some cases the rain waste falling upon roofs, yards, areas, and courts. We may distinguish street sewers and house sewers, the former being laid in the public streets, and intended for all the houses and lots composing a city block or blocks, the latter being the lateral branches for each building.

Shaft: (A) An upright object, high and comparatively small in horizontal dimensions. The term is applied to a building, as when a tower is said to be a plain shaft; to an architectural member, as when a high building is said to present a more elaborate basement and a less adorned shaft above; or to a single stone, an obelisk, menhir, cathstone, or the like. Even a classical column like "Pompey's Pillar," made up of capital, shaft, and base, is called in popular writing "a tall shaft." In modern usage, often, a straight enclosed space, as a well extending through the height of a building, or through several stories, for the passage of an elevator, to give light to interior rooms, or the like. Commonly, in combination, as elevator shaft; light shaft. (B) Specifically, the principal part of a column; that which makes up from two-thirds to nine-tenths of its height, and which is comparatively simple and uniform in treatment from end to end. The shaft of an Egyptian column was often diminished in size at the bottom, like the under side of a cup, and set without a base; then tapering to the neck. In Mycenaen art the shaft was often smallest at bottom, increasing in size upward by an even taper. This form has its prototype in the trunks of certain palm trees, which, when used as veranda posts and the like, are of very decorative. The shafts of Doric columns of the sixth century B.C. are about six times as high as they are in greatest diameter, and have an entasis showing a very visible curve. In the earlier Middle Ages, classical columns were so often taken for the new buildings, that their forms were inevitably copied in new work, but the result of Romanesque work, in making common the semi-cylindrical buttress piers within and without brought in a change, and free columns also were made cylindrical, without taper or swell. This custom prevailed without change throughout the epoch of Gothic architecture; and was only replaced, not modified, by the reintroduction of classical forms in the fifteenth and sixteenth centuries.

Shearing Weight: That kind of breaking weight or force which acts by shearing i.e. by pushing one portion of a member or material past the adjoining part, as by a pair of shears.

Sheathing Board: A board prepared for sheathing purposes, often with tongue and groove for jointing.

Sheathing Paper: A coarse paper specially prepared in various grades and laid with a lap under clapboards, shingles, slates, etc., to exclude weather, or between the upper and under flooring, for deafening. When made with asbestos or with magneso-calcite it is used for fireproofing.

Sheathing: A covering of boards, plywood or paneling etc. applied to the exterior rafters, joists or studs to strengthen the structure. In carpentry, a covering or lining to conceal a rough surface or to cover a timber frame. In general, any material, such as tin, copper, slate, tiles, etc., prepared for application to a structure, as covering.

Sheetrock: Gypsum plasterboard placed between paper.

Shell: (A) A furniture design motif. (B) A thin self-supporting member.

Shiplap: A joint that overlaps and joins two boards.

Shooting Board: (A) A slab of wood or metal used by carpenters, and provided with a device for holding an object while it is being shaped for use. (B) An inclined board fitted to slide material from one level to another.

Shoulder: The projection or break made on a piece of shaped wood, metal, or stone, where its width or thickness is suddenly changed, as at a tenon or rebate, the break being usually at right angles.

Shutter: A movable screen, cover, or similar contrivance to close an opening, especially a window. In the United States the term is commonly made to include all varieties of hinged and swinging blinds, as well as any solid or nearly solid structure to close an opening tightly at the outside. These latter would not be spoken of as blinds.

Siding: The covering, or material for covering, the exterior walls of a frame building, and forming the final finished surface, as distinguished from the sheathing, on which, when used, the siding is nailed.

Sill: A horizontal member at the base of a framed wall or at the bottom of a door frame or window opening.

Single Hung: Secured to one side or at one point only, as a sash which is hung by one cord, pulley, and weight. This plan is followed where a window is divided by a mullion which for any reason is to be made as slender as possible. A solid mullion being put in place, the two sliding sashes are each hung on the outer edge alone, the single weight being heavy enough to counterbalance the sash. It is usually necessary to insert rollers of some kind in the other stile of each sash to prevent their binding or sticking.

Skeleton Construction: Framework construction with a non-loadbearing outer covering. That which depends for its strength upon a skeleton; especially, in modern building beginning about 1885, a manner of building in which, while the exterior is of masonry, the whole structure is of iron or steel which supports the exterior walls as well as the roof. It is common to carry these exterior walls by means of cantilevers upon which one story or two stories of such walls are built up at a time; so that the structure may be completed and the roof put on before any part of the walls are in place. The walls may even be built in the tenth story before those of the eighth and ninth stories are completed, and so on.

Skew: Any member cut or set so as to present a sloping surface; especially for other necessary parts of a structure to butt against, as in a gable or the abutment of an arch.

Skewback: The portion of an abutment which supports an arch.

Skirting: An edging attached to the base of an interior wall.

Skylight: A glazed aperture in a roof, whether a simple glazed frame set in the plane of a roof, or a structure surmounting a roof with upright or sloping sides and perhaps an independent roof; the entire structure consisting wholly, or in large part, of glazed frames. In its more elaborate forms, a skylight may be constructed as a Lantern, or may have the semblance of a dormer window from which it is sometimes hardly to be distinguished. The term is, however, only applicable to such lights when overhead, i.e. located decidedly above, rather than at the sides of, the space immediately covered by the roof, although, perhaps, extending considerably down the lateral slopes of the roof. The frame is either of wood, or, preferably, of metal, braced or tied with iron rods.

Skyscraper: A multi-story building. They are constructed with a steel frame and curtain walls.

Slab: (A) A concrete floor set between walls or beams. (B) Any piece of material of considerable breadth and little thickness as compared to its length; more specifically, an outside plank as sawn from a log, having one rounded side and consequently of very unequal thickness. Except in the last sense the term is more frequently applied to stone than to other materials.

Slat: A flat and thin board or strip, especially if relatively narrow, usually of wood.

Slate: In building, Roofing Slate; that is to say, a fissile variety of argillite used mainly for roofing and, in more solid masses, for sinks, floor tiles, mantels, and the like. Roofing Slate is obtained by splitting the larger masses into thin slabs, which are then trimmed to certain standard dimensions. It was formerly divided in Great Britain into regular sizes known by arbitrary names. The sizes most often used are Countess, 10" x 20", and Duchess, 12" x 24". Other sizes are given as follows:-- Double, 7" x 13", Empress, 16" x 26". Lady, 8" x 16", Imperial, 24" x 30", Viscountess, 9" x 18", Rag, 24" x 36", Marchioness, 11" x 22", Queen, 24" x 36", Princess, 14" x 24". These terms have never been common in the United States. It is more usual to specify the sizes, which do not vary greatly. Thus, 8" x 16" is a good size for smaller surfaces, and 10" x 20" for large slopes of a roof. The varieties of slate are very great, and the preference for this or that quarry has varied from time to time, partly according to the color in vogue or called for by the building in question, and partly by the favor shown to a particular surface with or without glass and the like. Purple, green, and red are the common colors, and each of these colors is often very agreeable; moreover, it has been found easy to make somewhat effective patterns of their combination. On the other hand, the very darkest slate, that which approaches black, is preferred by many architects, and some of the best qualities of slate are of this color.

Slatehanging: Overlapping shingles made from slate. Used as exterior wall covering.

Slating: The applying of roofing slate to the sheathing boards or battens of strips which are nailed to the rafters. As the slating must overlap for a definite proportion of its length, the distance apart of the places for nailing can be determined beforehand. Thus, if slates 24 inches long are used, and if it be required that each slate overlap the one below it for 14 inches (leaving 10 inches "to the weather" in each course) then the rows of nails will be 10 inches apart. Nails may be driven near the center of each slate or near the head; it is rare that both methods are used, as two nails to a slate of ordinary size is considered sufficient. Nails should be of copper or be in some way protected by a non-corrosive metal composition, and the holes through which they are driven must be made in advance, which is done usually by the sharp point of the slater's hammer.

Slype: A covered passage in a monastic church connecting the transept and the chapter house.

Socket: A depression or cavity, shaped to receive and hold in place the foot of a column or beam, or the end of a bolt; or, in the case of heavy doors of the like, a revolving pivot.

Sod: The thin layer of soil matted together by the roots of grass and other small herbs which forms the surface of a lawn or grassy field; also, with the article, a small piece of this layer. "Turning the First Sod" is a ceremony akin to laying the corner stone.

Soffit Cusps: Cusps extending from the soffit of and arched head.

Soffit: The under side of a structure, especially of comparatively limited extent. Thus the under side of an arch or lintel and the sloping surface beneath a stair would be called soffits.

Solarium: A sun porch or terrace.

Solea: The pathway projecting from the bema to the ambo in a Byzantine church.

Spire: A tall pyramidal, polygonal or conical structure rising from a roof or tower and terminating in a point.

Splay: Any surface, larger than a Chamfer or a Bevel, making an oblique angle with another surface; specifically said of the oblique jamb of an opening as in a window or doorway.

Spline: (A) A thin, narrow board, corresponding generally to boards used for ceiling, and the like. (B) Same as Loose Tongue. (C) In drawing, a thin strip of some elastic, flexible material, used as a guide in drawing curves, by being bent to the desired form and held in place by weights or pins.

Spring: (A) The line of plane at which the curve of an arch or vault leaves the upright or impost. (B) Resilience, as of a floor; its elasticity when compressed.

Spring: To leave its impost by rounding upward and outward, said of an arch or vault. In making elevation drawings and section drawings, the horizontal plane at which this takes place is represented by a horizontal line; hence, the common term, Springing Line, which is used even when the building itself is under consideration, as when it is said by a person looking at a vault: The springing line is about nine feet above the pavement.

Springing Line: The horizontal line from which an arch rises.

Spur Stone: A stone projecting from the angle of a corner to prevent traffic damage.

Square, Carpenters': A steel implement forming a right angle with a shorter and a longer area, each divided into feet and inches or other measurements.

Square: (A) An open space, generally more or less rectangular, in a town, formed at the junction of two or more streets, or by the enlargement of one for a short distance; especially, such a place provided with a park or parks. (B) Same as Block (C) An instrument intended primarily for laying outright angles, consisting usually of two arms fixed, or capable of being accurately adjusted, perpendicularly to each other.

Square: To provide by an instrument, or otherwise, that the angles of a piece of work or material are right angles; or to ascertain the amount of their deviation from right angles.

Squinch: A small arch or system of arches built across an interior corner of a room to support a load such as a dome or tower.

Squint: A small oblique opening in a wall. Used in churches to afford a view of the altar from otherwise unaccessible areas.

Stability: As applied to structures, the property of remaining in equilibrium without change of position, although the externally applied force may deviate to a certain extent its mean amount of position. The conditions of equilibrium of a structure are these: (1) That the forces exerted on the whole structure by external bodies shall balance each other. The external forces are the force of gravity, causing the weight of the structure, the pressures exerted against it by bodies not forming part of it, and the supporting forces, or resistances of the foundations. (2) That the forces exerted on each piece of a structure shall balance each other. These forces are the weight, the external load, and the resistances, or stresses, exerted at the joints of the piece. (3) That the forces exerted upon each of the parts into which the pieces of a structure can be conceived to be divided shall balance each other. That is the stress exerted at the ideal surface of

division between the part in question and the other parts of the piece. (4) Stability consists in the fulfillment of the first and second conditions of equilibrium under all variations of load within given limits. Strength consists in the fulfillment of the third.

Stadium: A large sports arena or building. Usually open to the air. A running track in ancient Greece.

Stage Door: A door giving access to the stage and to that portion of a theater which is for the use of the actors and other employees.

Stained glass: Glass that is chemically treated and then fired to achieve the desired color.

Stair, Back: Any stair situated at the rear, that is, at the back, of a building, as for domestic service or other subordinate purpose. Hence, any retired and unimportant stair for a similar use, wherever situated.

Stair, Box: One made with two closed strings, so that it has a boxlike form of construction, and may be more or less completely finished before being set up on the site.

Stair, Cockle: From Cochlea; a helical or corkscrew stair.

Stair, Dog-leg; Dog-legged: A half turn stair consisting of two parallel flights, their strings and hand rails being in the same vertical plane. The hand rail of the lower flight commonly butts against the under side of the string of the upper flight, there being no well hole.

Stair, Geometrical: One which is constructed without the use of newels at the angles or turning points. The intersecting strings and hand rails are, therefore, usually joined by means of short curved portions called wreaths.

Stair, Newel; Newelled: One constructed with newels at the angles to receive the ends of the strings, as distinguished from a geometrical stair. The term is sometimes, with no apparent reason, limited to a dog-legged stair.

Stair, Open Newelled: A newelled stair which is built around a well; apparently, a term adapted to distinguish such a stair, which is "open" as regards the existence of a well, from a dog-legged stair, which has no well. Each is newelled.

Stair, Open Riser: One in which there is no riser in the sense of a solid board, metal casting, or the like, and the whole rise between tread and tread is left open. When this arrangement is followed in costly staircases of elaborate buildings, it is usually to allow light to pass, as from a window.

Stair, Screw: A circular stair; especially, one in which the steps radiate from a vertical post or newel.

Stair, Straight: One which rises in one direction only, without turns.

Stair, Water: Stairs or steps communicating between any water level, as of a river, lake, or harbor, and the land, for convenience of embarkation or debarkation.

Stair, Winding: Any stair constructed wholly or chiefly with winders.

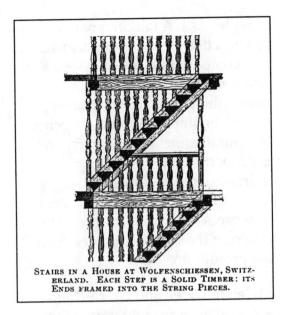

STAIRS IN A HOUSE AT WOLFENSCHIESSEN, SWITZ-ERLAND. EACH STEP IS A SOLID TIMBER: ITS ENDS FRAMED INTO THE STRING PIECES.

Staircase: (A) Properly, the structure containing a stair; a stair together with its enclosing walls. (B) Improperly, but in common usage, a stair or series of stairs; i.e., the complete mechanical structure of a stair or set of stairs with its supports, hand rails and other parts.

Stairway: Three or more risers constitute a stairway.

Stall: Carved wooden or stone seats placed in rows.

Stanchion: A vertical supporting member.

Starling: A pointing projection on the pier of a bridge used to break wave action.

Statuary: That form of sculpture which deals with figures in the round as distinguished from figures in relief, especially with figures of the human body complete, either singly or in groups. Such figures are used in architecture in two general ways. (1) In immediate connection with the building, as in cathedral porches of the thirteenth century, and commonly in niches and under canopies. (2) Set upon a building, but without apparent connection with its architectural design. Thus, in the pediment of a Greek temple the statues were designed for their place as so far above the eye and likely to be seen from so great a horizontal distance; but the tympanum of the pediment is used merely as a convenient background and the geison as a convenient shelf to support them. A similar arrangement seems to have existed in Roman theaters and amphitheaters, where the great open arches of the structure which supported the rising tiers of seats were often occupied by statues and groups well seen against the comparatively dark interior. In memorial arches, statues are set upon ressauts of the main order, and thus relieved against the attic. In the Renaissance and post-Renaissance styles statues appear against the sky ranged upon the pedestals of the parapet, as in the library of S. Mark in Venice, and the great colonnade by Bernini in the Piazza S. Pietro at Rome. This last-named arrangement involves the difficulty that the light of the sky eats into the outline of the statue, which can hardly be seen clearly unless illuminated by the sun from behind the spectator, or unless seen against a very somber background of clouds. It is partly to avoid this that there has been a partial return, as in highly decorated buildings in the United States, to the front of the attic as a place for statues; and other buildings have porticoes of slight projection chiefly to afford the same opportunity.

Stave Church: A timber framed church. It is a form of construction used in Scandinavian churches dating from the mid eleventh century onward.

Stay: Anything that stiffens or helps to maintain a frame or other structure, as a piece of timber or iron acting as a strut or brace; or a tie of any material.

Steeple: (A) A tall ornamental construction surmounting a tower and composed usually of a series of features superimposed and diminishing upward, as the steeples of Sir Christopher Wren's churches, in contradistinction to a spire, which is properly a tall pyramid uninterrupted by stories or stages. (B) A tower terminated by a steeple in sense A, or by a spire, the term covering the whole structure, from the ground up.

Stele: In Greek and Greco-Roman art, a pillar or upright monument composed of one or two stones and simple in its outline and general character, although it may be adorned with very elaborate carving. The more common forms were a slender cylinder, and a flat slab, higher and more narrow than a modern gravestone. These were set up as boundary stones; thus a law, or edict, or a treaty between two nations, would be recorded in an inscription upon a stele set up in an appropriate place. In some cases a sunken panel is filled by a bas-relief of a few figures, such as some in the Acropolis at Athens. The largest stelai known were erected on the graves of individuals, and these were sometimes sculptured with superb bas-reliefs, like those found in the graveyard at the Dipylon at Athens, and now in the Central Museum there. (Also written stela.)

Stereobate: A mass of masonry used as a base of a wall or series of columns.

Stile, Diminished; Diminishing: In a glazed door, a stile whose upper part above the middle rail is narrower than the lower part, in order to admit of a sash wider than the panelling below.

Stile, Gunstock: A diminished stile in which the reduction in width is made by a long slope, usually of the whole width of the lock rail.

Stile, Hanging: (A) In the framing of a door, a hinged casement window, or the like, that stile to which the hinges are secured, and by which, therefore, the door, etc., is hung to the jamb or doorpost. (B) Same as Pulley Stile.

Stile, Pulley: That surface of the box frame of a window, against which the sashes slide up and down; it receives its name from the sash pulleys which are set into it near the top, and through which the sash cords or chains are passed.

Stile, Shutting: In a hinged door, the stile opposite the hanging stile, being that one which strikes the rebate of the jamb when the door is shut.

Stile: Any plane surface forming a border. Specifically, in carpentry work and in joinery, one of the plane members of a piece of framing, into which the secondary members or rails are fitted by mortise and tenon, as in panelling. In framed doors, and the like, it is nearly always a vertical member.

Stilted: Raised higher than is normal, or usual, or seeming to be so raised, a term almost wholly limited to the arch, which is said to be stilted when the curve does not spring at or close to the top of the capital or of the molded or otherwise strongly marked impost. The term is extremely vague, as many arches have no architecturally marked impost, and as it is considered an error to start the curve immediately upon such an impost in any case; but those arches are called stilted which have a vertical jamb or intrados below the curve more than about one quarter of their total rise. Thus, fig. 1 shows an arch whose rise is one half its span; its springing line is raised above the moldings of the impost by nearly 1 1/2 times its span, and hence it is said to be much stilted.

Stone: (A) The material of which rocks are composed. (B) A fragment of a rock. (C) Any aggregate of mineral matter, natural or artificial, as in the terms "precious stone," "artificial stone." The kinds of stone utilized for purposed of construction or for general interior decorative, monumental, or art work, may be roughly grouped under five general heads ; granites, sandstones, marbles, limestones, and slates. The term "granite" in its strict scientific sense, is made to include only a class of eruptive rocks, consisting essentially of quartz and feldspar, with usually minerals of the hornblende or mica group, and which are consequently known as hornblende or mica granites. They are tough, hard rocks, massive and strong, of a pronounced granular structure, and vary in color through all shades of gray; pink and red colors are, however, not uncommon.

Stoop: A small residential entrance platform.

Stops: Stone, wood, etc. projections at the ends of masonry courses or molding used to butt terminate the course or moldings.

Story: The space between the upper surface of a floor and the upper surface of the floor above or between the floor and roof of a building.

Straightedge: (A) A ruler used by draughtsmen for ruling long lines for which the T-square cannot be conveniently employed; e.g. the converging lines of a large perspective drawing. It is usually of light, hard wood, but hard rubber and celluloid are also used. (B) An implement used in building, for various purposes. For laying off long lines and for testing the evenness of a plane surface of plaster or stone, a thoroughly seasoned board with an edge planed perfectly true is employed. For testing levels a long, wide board is used, having the lower edge perfectly true and the middle part of the back or upper edge parallel to it; from this part the back tapers somewhat to either end. It is used by setting the lower edge on the surface or surfaces to be tested, and applying the spirit-level to the middle of the back.

Strain Diagram; Polygon: A geometrical diagram used in the graphical method of determining the strains in a framed structure, such as a truss. The given loads or other outer forces are represented in amount and direction by a series of lines; other lines are plotted to the same scale corresponding in direction to the respective members of the structure. On completion of the polygon, these latter may be directly measured by scale on the drawing. The process is similar to that employed in the Polygon, and the Parallelogram, of Forces.

Strain: The deformation or change of shape of a body as the result of a Stress.

Stress: The resistance of a change in shape or size that is caused by an external force.

Stressed-skin Construction: Construction in which the outer skin or shell acts with the frame members to for a structurally strong unit.

Stressed-skin Panel: A panel of outer materials such as plywood fasted over a frame or core and forming a unitized structural member.

Strings: Two sloping members which carry the ends of treads and risers of a staircase.

Strip Development: A continuous string of houses or building along a road or street.

Stucco: A finish for walls made from sand, lime and cement mixed with water. It can be smooth or textured. Any material used as a covering for walls and the like, put on wet and drying hard and durable. Plaster when applied to walls in the usual way is a kind of stucco, and the hard finish is almost exactly like fine Roman stucco except that it is applied in only one thin coat instead of many. Vitruvius speaks of three coats mixed with sand and three coats mixed with marble dust, but does not give the thickness of the coats, nor, what would answer the same purpose, how wet the mixture was made. He speaks of well-finishing stucco shining so as to reflect the images falling upon it, and states that persons used to get slabs of plaster from ancient walls and used them for tables, the material being so beautiful in itself. The term is generally applied to out-of-door work. Even in modern fireproof buildings the decorative use of fine plastering to replace woodwork, as for dadoes and the like, is not in the United States called stucco, but takes the name of the material used, generally a proprietary name. The term is used commonly for rough finish of outer walls. The practical value of stucco is very great as being so nearly impervious to water; thus, an excellent wall three stories high, or even higher, may be built with 8 inches of brick on the inner side, 4 inches of brick on the outer side, an air space of 2 or 4 inches across which the outer and the inner walls are well tied, and two coats of well-mixed and well-laid stucco on the exterior, this being finally painted with oil paint.

Stud: (A) A relatively small projecting member as a boss, a small knob, a salient nailhead; either for ornamental or mechanical purpose. (B) Vertical framing members for interior and exterior wall construction. Often 2x4's of wood or metal.

Studio: (A) The working room of an artist, preferably arranged in north latitude, to receive north light and especially free from cross lights. (B) By extension from the above, any large apartment fitted as a working room, especially for more or less artistic employments, as photography and designing of all sorts.

Stupa: A Buddhist religious structure.

Style: (A) Character; the sum of many peculiarities, as when it is said that a certain building is in a spirited style. By extension, significance, individuality; especially in a good sense and imputed as a merit, as in the expression, "Such a building has style." (B) A peculiar type of building, of ornament, or the like, and constituting a strongly marked and easily distinguished group or epoch in the history of art; thus we say that in Europe the Romanesque style prevailed from the fall of the Western Empire until the rise of the Gothic style; but we also say that during the Romanesque period such minor styles as the Latin style, the Rhenish or West German style, the Norman Romanesque style, more vigorous in England than even in the country of its origin, and the Tuscan round-arched style, as in the church of Samminiato al Monte, were all in existence successively, or at the same time.

Stylobate: The substructure of a colonnade.

Subarch: One of two or more minor arches beneath and enclosed by an outer arch, as in Gothic tracery, or in the simpler forms of Italian domestic architecture.

Subflooring: A rough base for a finished floor which rests on joists.

Superimposed Orders: Multiple classical orders used in a multi-story or colonnaded building. Used in the following order: Doric, Ionic and Corinthian.

Superstructure: A structure raised upon another structure, as a building upon a foundation, basement, or substructure.

Swan-neck: An ogee-shaped member.

Symmetry: In architecture and decorative art, the balance of part by part; a balance which may be precise repetition, or repetition in counterpart, or may deviate very widely from that, as it involves merely the supposed equivalent value of one part to another.

T

T-Square: A drafting tool used to draw lines parallel to the drawing board front edge. It is snuggled tightly against the drawing board edge and the pencil is drawn across the plastic edge to make a straight and parallel line. Angled and perpendicular lines are constructed with a triangle. A wooden T-square with a clear plastic edge is the preferred one for drafting.

Tabernacle: A canopied container or structure used to house a sacramental or religious relic or object. A tent or free-standing canopy.

TABLET IN THE VON DER LINDE HOLM, SWEDEN

Tablet: (A) A small slab or panel, usually a separate piece, set into or attached to a wall or other larger mass, usually intended to receive an inscription. (B) A horizontal coping or capping of a wall, sometimes called Tabling.

Tablinum: A room with one side open to the atrium of a Roman building.

Tamp: To ram an earth surface, so as to harden it and form a floor, or the bottom of a trench to make it fit to receive foundations.

Tas-de-charge: The lowest course of an arch or vault. It is laid horizontally and bonded into the wall.

Tear strength: Resistance to the propagation of an existing tear.

Tebam: The speakers' or readers' dais in a synagogue.

Technical pen: The basic ink drawing instrument. It is easy to use and comes in many line widths for various needs. It produces a uniform line width. A good basic set would include a 00 (very fine), 0, 2 1/2; then add 000, 1, 2, and 4. A good sketching instrument to use when you occasionally need to draft lines in ink for presentations and the like is 00.

Temper: (A) To mix, moisten, and knead clay, so as to bring it to proper consistency to form bricks, pottery, terra cotta, etc., preliminary to hardening by fire. (B) To bring a metal, as steel, to a proper degree of hardness and elasticity, by alternately heating and suddenly cooling the metal, its color, by those processes, gradually changing from light yellow to dark blue, the metal becoming harder at each stage. (C) To toughen and harden glass by plunging it at a high temperature into an oleaginous bath, under the process invented by M. de la Bastie, or by heating and suddenly cooling it, according to the Siemen process. (D) To mix and knead lime and sand and water, in such proportions as to make mortar for masonry or plastering.

Template: (A) A paper or cardboard pattern used by installers as a guide for cutting carpet for areas having complicated or unusual shapes. (B) A stone block set on top of a brick wall to carry the weight of joists or trusses.

Temple: A religious building, usually a building of worship or cultic practice.

Tenia: Molding along the top of the architrave in the Doric order.

Tenon: The cutting of the end of a rail, mullion, sill, or beam to form a projection of smaller transverse section than the piece, with a shoulder, so that it may be fitted into a corresponding hold or mortise in another piece.

Tensile strength: The breaking strain of yarns or fabrics. A high tensile strength indicates strong yarns or fabrics.

Tension Bar: A bar or rod to which a strain of tension is applied, or by which it is resisted.

Tension Member Piece: In a framework, truss, or the like, a piece calculated to resist strains of tension; as a tie.

Tension: A force that causes a body to become longer or pull apart.

Terminal: In Latin, having to do with the Roman god Terminus. A Terminal Figure is a decorative figure in which a head, or a head and bust, or the human figure to the waist and including the arms, is finished by a block, prism-like, or shaped like a reversed truncated cone, and either plain or decorated severely. These figures are thought to have been used originally for statues of Hermes as god of roads and boundaries corresponding to the Roman Terminus. Ancient Greco-Roman examples are sometimes arranged for two heads attached at the back and facing in opposite directions. A Terminal Pedestal is a pedestal prepared for a bust, so that the two together would be a Terminal Figure.

Terminal: The ornamental finish, or termination, of an object, corresponding sometimes nearly to Finial or to Acroterium, but applied to minor and subordinate uses. Thus, the carved end of a bench, as in a church, is called by this name.

Terra Cotta: Hard baked pottery, especially that which is used in architecture or in decorative art of large scale. It may be left with its natural brown surface unglazed and uncolored, or it may be painted as was customary among the Greeks, or it may be covered with a solid enamel of grave or brilliant colors. In parts of Italy the architecture of

the later Gothic style and of the early Renaissance is marked by the free use of terra cotta. In the nineteenth century its use was largely revived, and in England from 1860, and in the United States from about 1880, it has been freely employed in connection with bricks of similar or agreeable contrasting color for the exterior of buildings.

Terrace: A series of attached housed. A level walk attached or adjacent to a building.

Terrazzo: Marble chips mixed with cement mortar on site then ground and polished. Used as a flooring material.

Tetrastyle: A portico with four frontal columns.

Thatch: Roof covering of straw or reeds. Such a covering was generally 12 inches thick in England, and is said to have been better when several inches thicker. Wheat straw carefully combed and cleared of short pieces was considered the best material, except where good rushes were available. Thatch was often whitewashed as a partial preventive against fire, and even plastering or clay applied in a thick coat was used for the same purpose.

Thrust: A force which pushes and tends to compress, crush, displace, or overturn a body; as the thrust of an arch is the force tending to push back or overturn the pier or abutment. In an arch it may also be defined as the horizontal component of the reaction of the abutment, and, therefore, uniform throughout the arch.

Tie Beam: In common wooden framed construction, especially in roofing, the large horizontal piece which crosses from wall to wall, or between any points of support, forming the lowest member of a truss, and into which the rafters are framed, its center being often kept from sagging by a king-post. The main horizontal transverse timber which carries the feet of the principals at wall-plate level.

Tie Rod: A rod, usually of iron, used as a tie to prevent the spreading of an arch, or of a piece of framing in wood or iron. In the commonest form it replaces the tie beam, the king-post, or other simple member intended to resist tension.

Tie: Anything which is used to resist a pull, as to prevent the spreading of the two sides of a roof, the separating of the two solid parts of a hollow wall, the collapsing of a trussed beam, and the like. Much used in composition.

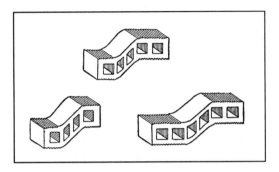

Tile: (A) Primarily, a piece of solid material used for covering a roof of a building. Roof tiles may be either flat or may be of different sections, so as to produce ridges and valleys, and so that one form covers the joints between tiles of another form, as will be explained below. (B) Any slab of hard material, large or small, but especially one of many rather small pieces, used together to form roofing, flooring, wall facing, or the like. Much the greater number of tiles have always been made of baked clay in some form; but marble, stone, and other materials are used. (C) By extension, and because of the application of the name to all pieces of baked clay used for accessories to building, a piece of drain pipe; one section of a continuous tube. In this sense often called Draining Tile or Drain Tile.

(D) A piece of hard material, especially of baked clay, used for any purpose whatever, even for the preserving of written records, as in the case of those libraries entirely composed of inscribed tiles which have been found in Mesopotamia.

Timber: Wood, whether growing or cut, of such quality and size as fit it for use in building; excluding that which has been cut up into planks or boards, and, in the United States, that cut smaller than about 6" X 6".

Torsion: The act or result of twisting, as of a timber so distorted in drying or under some especial strain.

Torsional Strength: The strength of a member or material to resist a torsional force; i.e. a force tending to separate or break by twisting.

Torus: A bold projecting molding, convex in section, forming generally the lowest member of a base over the plinth, especially of a column or pilaster. When two tori are used, separated by a Scotia with fillets, the parts being of normal relative size, the combination forms an Attic Base.

Tower House: A fortified house. Common in Scottish architecture.

Trabeated: In Greek architecture, a building of post-and-lintel construction.

Tracery: Decoration made of lines or of narrow bands and fillets, or of more elaborately molded strips, but always without, or with but little, representation of natural objects. By extension, and because the word became identified with the subdivisions of a window, design in pierced patterns, in which the openings show dark on light from without and light on dark from within. The term when used without qualification has come to mean Gothic window tracery exclusively; but precisely similar tracery was used contemporaneously in stone relief, in wood carving, as on doors and pieces of furniture, and in pierced, cast, and wrought metal. Tracery of totally different character is found in scrollwork of the simpler kinds, as in Roman so-called Arabesques, Strapwork, and Interlaced Ornament, and in Northern sculpture of the early Middle Ages.

Tracing House: The room or shed where medieval masons drafted the details of the buildings, carvings and moldings prior to construction.

Tracings: In times past, architects paid people to make "tracings" of their original drawings to give to the contractors. This process was supplanted by the "blueprinting" process and left us with the term "tracing" which is still used to describe that original drawing on translucent paper. The "blueprinting" process itself has since been largely replaced by a much more inexpensive process called *Diazo*.

Transenna: A marble lattice screen in early churches.

Transept: The cruciform church's lateral arm.

Transition: In architectural style, the passing from one style to another. This process is always slow, and is marked by the designing of buildings, or parts of buildings, in which the new style is not yet fully in control. This will be more visible in buildings of secondary importance, though occasionally a monument of great size and cost will show the changing style. The transition from Romanesque to Gothic is marked by the architectural style of domestic buildings throughout Europe, and that from Gothic to Renaissance includes the whole interesting florid Gothic of France and Germany; while in England the same changes go on at a still slower pace, that of the sixteenth century extending indefinitely into the time of the Stuart monarchs.

Transom Bar: A comparatively slight and subordinate transom; especially, in modern usage, a bar separating a fanlight from the opening below.

Transom: A hinged window found over a door or another window. A horizontal bar across a window opening or panel. A horizontal bar of stone, metal, or wood, as distinguished from a Mullion; especially one across a door or window opening near the top.

Traverse: Any member, or structure, set or built across an interior or an opening; especially (A) A screen, railing, or other barrier, used to keep away intruders, to allow passage from one place to another by an official or dignitary, or to conceal anything. (B) A Transom, or the horizontal member of a Chambranle.

Tread: (A) That part of a step in a stairway, of a doorsill, or the like, upon which the foot rests, as distinguished from the riser. The term applies equally to the upper surface along, and to the plank, slab of marble or slate, or thin casting of iron, in those staircases which each step is not a solid mass. (B) The horizontal distance from one riser to the next. Thus, a stair is said to have 12 1/2' tread, that being the whole distance which a person moves horizontally in ascending one step. This distance is measured without regard to the nosing, which, where it exists, projects beyond the riser in each case.

Triangle: A drawing instrument in the form of a mathematical right-angled triangle cut from a flat thin piece of wood, hard rubber, celluloid, or metal, or framed of three strips; used for drawing parallel lines at any given angle by sliding it along the fixed blade of a T-square, straight edge, or the like. The right-angled side serves for lines perpendicular to the blade, the oblique side for inclined lines. The commonest forms of triangle have acute angles both of 45 degrees or one of 30 degrees and one of 60 degrees; but special forms are made with other angles for lettering and

other special purposes. Also, called Set Square.

Triangulation: The achievement of stability in an assembly of triangular struts and ties.

Tribune: A raised platform or dais. The apse of a basilica.

Triclinium: A dining room in a Roman house.

Triforium: An arcade opening on the nave of a church.

Triglyphs: Blocks that separate the metopes in a Doric frieze.

Trilithon: A prehistoric monument consisting of a megalithic lintel placed on two vertical stones.

Trim: The framing of a wall, door, window opening or around an architectural element.

Triumphal Arch: A monumental gateway built to commemorate a battle or other important public event. Common in Rome.

Triumphal Column: A monumental column built to commemorate a battle or other important public event. Common in Rome.

Trowel: (A) A mason's tool made of a thin plate of metal, approximately lozenge-shaped, always pointed at the end, and fitted with a handle; used for spreading and otherwise manipulating mortar in laying up masonry, and for breaking and trimming bricks. (B) A plasterer's tool, generally a small parallelogram of thin wood, with a handle underneath; used either like a pallet to hold putty or mortar, or to spread or float the last coat upon walls of ceilings. Masons use a tool of the same sort for kneading and mixing putty in pointing joints.

Truss, Howe: A bridge truss in which the struts are diagonal, crossing one another, and the chords are held together by vertical ties.

Truss, Pratt: A bridge truss in which the struts are vertical and the ties diagonal.

Truss, Scissor Beam: A roof truss in which the feet of the principal rafters are connected, each with a point on the upper half of the opposite rafter, by ties which cross at the middle like the two halves of a pair of scissors. It is a weak truss, fit for small spans only.

Truss, Warren: One with parallel chords between which the braces and ties are set at the same angle, so as to form a series of isosceles triangles.

Truss: A combination of rigid pieces, as posts and struts, with ties, so as to make a frame for spanning an opening or the like. Under Roof, Figs. 1 and 2 show a King-post Truss and a Queen-post Truss; Fig. 3 is also of a King-post Truss, but is not well shown, and Fig. 10 is a hammer Beam Truss, though not adequately framed; (Roof-Col 352, Vol III) but the other cuts are of roofs whose principals are not trusses, in a strict sense. A truss must be made up of triangles, as no other mathematical figure is fixed and immovable. The Howe, Pratt, and Warren trusses are used in building to carry large roofs where supporting uprights are to be avoided, as in a music hall or large modern church.

Turret: A small slender tower.

Tusking: Stones or masonry left protruding from a wall to attach another wall in the future.

U

Undercroft: An underground vaulted room.

Underpinning: (A) The rough walls or piers supporting the first floor timbers of a building without a cellar. The upper part of a foundation wall showing above the grade and under the water table, or ground sill. In New England often used for the masonry foundations, as in a house otherwise built of wood. (B) The material and labor used in replacing, in whole or in part, an old or infirm foundation wall with a new wall, or in extending with new material a wall already built to a lower and more stable bottom. The terms also applied to labor and material employed in the reconstruction of an old wall, so as to furnish a new and permanent bed for a stone or bearing for a beam.

Undressed timber: Unsanded timber.

Urinal: A toilet room convenience or plumbing fixture intended for men's use, and consisting of a trapped bowl, trough, or gutter, connected with a waste or drain pipe, and arranged with a flushing device similar to that for water-closets. By extension, the apartment in which this fixture is placed or fitted up.

V

Vanishing Point: In Perspective, a point toward which any series of parallel lines seems to converge.

Vanishing points: The point to which all parallel lines converge. All sets of parallel lines have their own vanishing point. In perspective drawing we establish vanishing points for 1, 2 and 3 point presentation but, in fact, there are an infinite number of actual vanishing points.

Vault, Groin: A curved line that forms when two vaults intersect.

Vaulting shaft: A vertical member which leads to the springer of a vault.

Veneer: A thin sheet or layer of wood, usually rotary cut, sliced or sawn from a log or flitch. Thickness may vary from 1/100' to 1/4".

Villa: An estate or large house on an estate. A country house.

Vimana: An Indian temple.

Vitruvian Opening: An Egyptian styled doorway with the inside edges sloping inward.

Volute: The spiral scroll on an Ionic, Composite or Corinthian capital.

Voussoir: A wedge-shaped stone or brick forming an element on and arch.

Vyse: A spiral staircase surrounding a central column.

W

Wainscot: A lower interior wall surface that contrasts with the wall surface above it. Unless otherwise specified, it shall be 4'-0" in height above the floor.

Wall arcade: A blind arcade.

Walls: Vertical partitions dividing one space from another or enclosing a space. They may or may not bear a load from above.

Ward: A castle courtyard.

Wattle and daub: An archaic wall construction made of lath or branches plastered with mud.

Wealden House: Medieval timber-framed house.

Weatherboarding: Horizontal overlapping board siding used in wood frame or timber construction.

Web: A bay or cell of a vault.

Westwork: The west end of a Romanesque church.

Wind Pressure: The force exerted by wind upon any part of a building. This is, generally, matter of inquiry and precaution only in the matter of high roofs, or spires; as the walls of an ordinary building when built in the common way are not affected by any winds but tornadoes or tropical hurricanes. The force of wind upon a roof is generally considered as a horizontal force, tending to push the roof over; but it really acts along a line normal to the sloping surface.

Winder: A step, more or less wedge-shaped in plan, adjusted to the angle or curve of a turn in a stair, as described under Step. As a winder cannot conform in width to the size assumed for the fliers, this regular spacing is usually, in good work, measured on the curve naturally followed by a person ascending with his hand on the rail along the well or newel side. This is usually taken as a curve parallel to the rail, and from 15 to 18 inches from it. The risers of such steps should not, in good work, radiate from a common center except in the case of a winding stair. It is more convenient, as well as safer, to cause them to converge somewhat before the actual turning place is reached, so that the fliers pass almost insensibly into the winders. The common plan in an ordinary stair, and one to be generally condemned, is to permit three, or even four, steps to occupy a quarter-pace, with risers radiating from a common point.

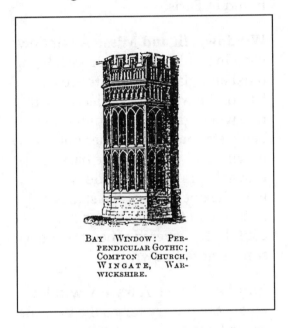

BAY WINDOW: PERPENDICULAR GOTHIC; COMPTON CHURCH, WINGATE, WARWICKSHIRE.

Window, Bay: Originally, a large window, often of many parts, or subdivisions. The word "bay" in its two senses, first, of a recess or opening, and second, of one of many subdivisions of a long building, seems to have suggested the use of the same term, "bay," for an enclosed structure which would form a recess, or opening, and which, by means of its projection from the exterior wall, would seem to constitute one

subdivision, or "bay," as seen from the exterior. This structure was then called bay window, and the term has no closer or more exact signification than is here explained.

The bay window is distinguished as a structure resting on the ground from the oriel window as a structure corbelled out from the wall of the building. Also a distinction has been attempted between bow window with a curved outline in its plan, and bay window with a broken or polygonal outline. As generally understood, in country houses and the like, the bay window is of the nature of an enclosed loggia by means of which a view can be had along the face of the walls on each side, and the sun can perhaps be let into a room which would otherwise not receive it; it may be two or three feet deep, or it may be as large as a moderate-sized room with a projection from the wall even greater than its measurement along the face of the wall. In some cases, the bay window is separated from the room which it adjoins by a decided break in the ceiling, as by an arch or transom, and the ceiling of the bay window may be lower than that of the room. In other cases the ceiling is continuous, and the bay window is really a prolongation, or widening, of the room.

Window, Blind: A non-functional window applied to a wall for decorative purpose or fenestration.

Window, Bull's Eye: A small round window.

Window, Catherine Wheel: Same as Rose Window.

Window, Compass: In England, a bay window of a semicircular or otherwise curved plan; rare or obsolete in the United States.

Window, Cross: A window with one mullion and one transom.

Window, Dormer: Originally a window of a dormer, .A In modern times a window in the vertical face of a relatively small structure projecting from a sloping roof. The vertical face may be a continuation of the wall carried up above the eaves. In common speech the term is applied to the whole structure, including the vertical side walls, which are usually triangular in shape, and the roof, which may be gabled, hipped, or of penthouse form. Cf. a similar use of the term Bay Window.

Window, Diocletian: Same as Venetian Window.

Window, French: A window similiar to a French window usually found in Paris.

Window, Hit and Miss: A window used in stables, the upper sash being fixed and glazed, while the lower half of the window is filled in with two wood gratings, the outer one being stationary, the inner one moving in a groove. The bars of the movable grating are made wider than the openings of the stationary one, so that these openings are completely covered when the inner sash is closed down.

Window, Jesse: A tracery window where the tracery forms the branches of the Jesse tree. The Jesse tree shows the genealogy of Christ ascending from Jesse.

Window, Laced: Window that are visually connected by coiored bricks.

Window, Lancet: A thin pointed window in the form of an arch.

Window, Lattice: A window with leaded diamond shaped lights. A hinged window as opposed to a sash window.

Window, Lowside: A window, usually very small, set much below the level of the larger windows, especially in a church, principally English. There is much dispute about the purpose of a lowside window in a church; all the ecclesiologists agree that it was not originally glazed, but closed probably by solid shutters, and it has been noted that a seat of solid material is often placed immediately within the opening. When the lowside window is very near the chancel, it may have been intended to afford a view of the altar from without; but these openings are found in all parts of the church.

Window, Offertory: Same as Lowside Window.

Window, Oriel: See Bay window.

Window, Palladian: Same as Venetian Window.

Window, Pede: A window in such a position with regard to another and larger window above as to be supposed to symbolize one of the feet of Christ.

Window, Rose: A circular window divided into compartments by mullions, forming tracery radiating from, or having more of less geometrical relations with, the center. They are especially frequent in French medieval architecture, where they occur as the characteristic central feature of the western fronts and transept, fronts which allow great size. They are distinguished by great beauty of detail, geometrical or flamboyant, according to the period of their construction. Some circular windows of the later medieval cathedrals of France hardly recognize the center as a generative point for the tracery.

Window, Transom: (A) A window divided by a transom into an upper and lower part. (B) A window above a transom, as in a doorway.

Window, Venetian: A window characteristic of the neoclassic styles having an arched aperture, flanked by a narrow, square-headed aperture on either side, separated by columns of pilasters.

Window, Wheel: A large circular window on which the radiation of tracery from the center is more or less distinctly suggested. It may be considered a variety of the Rose Window, in which the tracery is more distinctly committed to a spokelike arrangement. Also called Catherine Wheel Window.

Window, Wyatt: In Ireland, a square-headed Venetian Window, or a wide window divided into three openings by two mullions.

Window: An opening for the admission of light and sometimes of air into the interior of a building; and, by extension, the filling of this opening with glass, as usual in modern times, with the frame and sash, or casement, and their accessories. the term is usually confined to openings in vertical or nearly vertical surfaces, as walls. It is impracticable to distinguish in terms between the opening and the filling, as can be done between Doorway and Door.

Z

Zax: An implement used for cutting and pressing slates. It is usually a kind of hatchet, with a sharp point on the pole for perforating slate to receive a nail or pin.

Zoophorus: A frieze with animal figures.